FILM SCHEDULING

Or, How Long Will It Take To Shoot Your Movie?

SECOND EDITION

Ralph S. Singleton

The complete
step-by-step guide to
professional motion picture scheduling

LONE
EAGLE

FILM SCHEDULING Second Edition
Or, How Long Will It Take To Shoot Your Movie?

Copyright © 1984, 1991 by Ralph S. Singleton

LONE EAGLE PUBLISHING CO.
2337 Roscomare Road, Suite Nine
Los Angeles, CA 90077-1815
310/471-8066 • FAX 310/471-4969

Printed in the United States of America

Cover design by Heidi Frieder

First Printing, May 1984
Second Printing, January 1986
Third Printing, September 1987
Fourth Printing, January 1989
Fifth Printing, February 1991 - Second Edition
Sixth Printing, January 1992 - Second Edition

Library of Congress Cataloging in Publication Data

Singleton, Ralph S. (Ralph Stuart), 1940-
        FILM SCHEDULING, Or, How Long Will It Take To
Shoot Your Movie?
        Includes index.
        1. Moving Pictures — Production and direction —
Planning. I. Title. II Title: Film scheduling. III. Title: How long
will it take to shoot your movie?
PN1995.9.P7S58   1984   791.43'0232   84-5691
ISBN 0-943728-39-8

Material from "The Conversation" reproduced with permission from Francis F. Coppola.

FILM
SCHEDULING

For
Francis Coppola

TABLE OF CONTENTS

ACKNOWLEDGMENTS

I would like to thank those producers, production executives, production managers, first assistant directors and production accountants with whom I have worked and who have helped me over the years. Without their guidance, patience and friendship, this book would not have been possible. To name all those who have helped me over the years would fill another book, so I shall name just a few: Larry Albucher, Jacqueline Babbin, Jonathan Bernstein, Peter Cornberg, William Eustace, Paul Ganapoler, Wolfgang Glattes, David Golden, Sam Goldrich, George Goodman, Alex Hapsas, William Hassell, George Justin, Larry Kostroff, Charles McGuire, John Neukum, Stanley Neufeld, Charles Okun, Robert Relyea, Peter Scoppa, James Turner, Kenneth Utt, Herb Wallerstein and Ted Zachary.

A special thanks to (the late) Clark Paylow, the production manager of THE CONVERSATION.

A word of gratitude to Patrushka Mierzwa for her detailed notes on errors and omissions from the first version of this book.

One special individual guided this project from its formative period to its completion. Through her intelligence, perserverence and genuine belief in the idea, this book was born. There is no one I can give more thanks than Joan Vietor, my editor and publisher (and now, luckily, also my wife!)

Ralph S. Singleton
Los Angeles, California

FOREWORD

When Ralph Singleton and I first met each other as DGA trainees in New York, we both wondered why there was no adequate text book on film production. We vowed that once we became production managers and figured out what was going on, we'd write that book ourselves. Well, as you can see, Ralph has done it. And not only one book, but four: this one on scheduling, one on budgeting, a workbook and a dictionary.

Laying out a schedule for a film (or television project) is a crucial first step towards launching your project successfully. No film can be budgeted properly without a schedule. A schedule can provide you with ways to talk intelligently about your screenplay and to base critical decisions (actors, locations, weather, etc.) on reality rather than the fantasy induced by the euphoria of making the deal.

Many people want to jump right from *the deal* to *the budget.* Unless that budget has been derived from a detailed analysis of the screenplay, it will be just another piece of fiction. Just as a good script is the foundation for a well-received film, a well-thought-out schedule is the foundation for an on-budget production.

The motion picture business is fascinating and complicated. During the years that I worked as a production manager/assistant director, countless numbers of people would ask me how I learned to prepare a budget and shooting schedule. I learned the way most production people do—on the job. It is only in the last few years that colleges and universities have begun offering specific courses on film production. But even with the advent of these courses, the amount of material written by working professionals has been sorely lacking. There are dozens of books on acting, directing, screenwriting and even producing, but not on the logistics of film production. *Film Scheduling* answers the questions of how to transform written words into a blueprint —the shooting schedule. Ralph has been a production manager/assistant director on feature films and television shows, both large and small. He has taken these years of experience and put them into readable, understandable terms. This is the best book on film scheduling that I have read.

Film Scheduling would have been a terrific help when I was starting out. I heartily recommend it to anyone who wants to learn about motion picture production—from students to studio executives, film buffs to financiers.

Jonathan Sanger

AUTHOR'S NOTE

"*I t's been done this way for sixty years, and'll probably be done this way for the next sixty.*" That's the answer I got when I'd ask around to see if there were any new production/budget forms that made a little more sense than the ones that I'd been using. Production managing a motion picture is difficult enough without having to decipher and sift through the multitude of forms and formats available on the market today. None of those forms really offered a logical progression or any sort of standardization from script breakdown to budget. After many years of vowing to do something about it, and many hours of discussion with other production veterans, I decided to do something about it and designed a whole set of production and budget forms. You'll see some of them here, and some in *Film Budgeting,* but most of them are in *The Film Scheduling/Film Budgeting Workbook.* In later chapters, you'll learn about COLOR-CODING, and I think you'll be pleased to see how logical it makes things. The same color that is assigned to a category used when breaking down a script also carries through to the BUDGET FORM. The information on the BREAKDOWN SHEET is listed in the same order that it is on the budget form—less chance to miss something. The breakdown sheets themselves are printed on different color papers which correspond to the production strips—again, hopefully to save you time and reduce errors when you are trying to get ready for a production.

With this book, *Film Scheduling,* and the companion books, I hope to take some of the mystery out of film production management and streamline the process. It's taken a long time for this book to reach you. I'd love to hear your comments—praise or criticism—when you've finished. I'm also looking forward to seeing your name on the screen when future production credits roll.

R. S. S.

Note: Words in BOLD-FACE SMALL CAPS are defined in the glossary.

AUTHOR'S ADDITIONAL NOTE

Since the original publication of *Film Scheduling*, many changes have occurred in the film and television industry. One of the major changes has been the use of computers—from electronic storyboards, to computer-synthesized film scores, computerized film and videotape editing, and, as I cover in *Chapter Eleven*, computerized film scheduling. As many of us now cannot imagine life without our carphones and fax machines, soon computerized film scheduling become the standard.

Walt Gilmore, a fellow member of the Directors Guild of America, and experienced production manager, has lent his expertise to the analysis of the various programs on the market today. Follow his sage advice and check out several programs before deciding to buy.

Although *Film Budgeting* was seriously delayed due to work (and to those loyal telephoners who have plagued the publishing office—I apologize, and thank you for your continued reminders that you want these books), I think you will find it a good companion guide to *Film Scheduling*. Do keep your comments coming.

R.S.S.

I
INTRODUCTION

THE SIX STAGES OF PRODUCTION

1. Wild Enthusiasm
2. Total Confusion
3. Utter Despair
4. Search for the Guilty
5. Persecution of the Innocent
6. Promotion of the Incompetent

Anon.

There is an adage which says, "It only takes two things to make movies: time and money." But HOW MUCH TIME? and HOW MUCH MONEY? How to find the answers to the first question will be found in this book—how to find the answers to the second question in the companion volume, *Film Budgeting*.

Whether you are a **PRODUCER** or a **PRODUCTION MANAGER**, whether you are working on a studio picture or trying to get your own independent feature off the ground, your ability to succeed will depend on how well you can answer these two questions.

Scheduling a feature film is a three-part process:

1) breaking down the script,

2) preparing a production strip board, and

3) determining the final shooting schedule.

Perhaps two obvious questions should be answered now: 1) Why is it necessary to break down a script? and, 2) Isn't there an easier and more reliable method?

To answer the first question, it is necessary to break down a script in order to be able to budget it, and ultimately, finance it. Breaking down a script is the process of taking each and every element in the script, accounting for it and scheduling it in the most expedient and cost-effective manner. Once you have broken down a script and created the **PRODUCTION STRIP BOARD** and **SHOOTING SCHEDULE**, you will be able to move on to the next step: budgeting. Remember—if you cannot schedule a picture, you cannot budget it.

To answer the second question, yes, we feel that there is an easier and potentially more reliable method than the rather out-moded version of pick-up-sticks (the production strip board) which we still use today, and that method employs a computer. We say "potentially" because the human element is still the most important part of effective scheduling and budgeting a feature film. Micro-processors are being used in almost every other phase of motion picture making these days, and hopefully they will soon also be used by producers, production managers and **AUDITORS**. Although there are companies using computers for their SCRIPT BREAKDOWNS and production scheduling in addition to their budget preparation and daily accounting functions, the practice is not yet widespread enough to consider it the norm. Therefore, we have chosen to show you our version of the system which is currently in use.

Many of you have looked at a production strip board and wondered how in the world anyone could create something so complicated. Take heart. At first glance, analyzing how long and how much seems like an impossible task. It is complicated and it is time-consuming, but it is not impossible. Although time is of the essence, you are not in a race. The extra time you spend and the care you take in breaking down your script and preparing your strip board and budget will be worth it—well worth it. Problems which are overlooked or neglected in the early stages of pre-production have an uncanny tendency of showing up later on in the production . . . and they cost a lot more to handle when there is a cast and crew standing around waiting.

This book was designed to give you real-life filmmaking situations and then show you how we suggest you handle them. We are extremely fortunate in being able to use the entire screenplay of *Francis Ford Coppola's* Academy Award nominated film, THE CONVERSATION, and include it in its entirety in *The Film Scheduling Film/Budgeting Workbook.* Although there is no such thing as a *typical* screenplay, we feel that THE CONVERSATION involves some of the most difficult situations you as a production person might encounter. In its designed complexity, the script has characters developing from the very first page. Unfortunately, this is very rare. If in your work you try to compare most scripts with THE CONVERSATION they will fall way short of the mark. The more we analyzed this screenplay, the more apparent was the writer's genius. After spending over one year analyzing its construction in great detail in order to write this book, it was not difficult for us to understand why this screenplay was nominated for an Academy Award. A great film begins with a great screenplay. This screenplay remained fresh and alive for us, even after the twentieth reading.

When you begin to break down the script and prepare the strip board and later on learn how to prepare a budget in the book *Film Budgeting,* you will learn the steps to follow for a Union and Guild production. We will refer to the specific Union and Guild regulations and adhere to them. We want you to learn to be prepared for the most professional and most difficult situations. If you can prepare for the worst then chances are you might be pleasantly surprised in almost any other situation. For those of you wanting to adapt these techniques to 16mm and 8mm productions, the major changes will occur when it comes to budgeting—your scheduling techniques should remain the same.

We have designed this series of books to be used by everyone involved in or interested in being involved in motion picture production. There is no better method to learn how to schedule and budget a feature film than by actually doing it. *The Film Scheduling/Film Budgeting Workbook* contains the entire script of THE CONVERSATION, plus sample forms of everything you will need in scheduling and budgeting a feature film project. If you follow the steps outlined in *Film Scheduling* and *Film Budgeting* you will be able to produce your own production board and feature film budget.

In *Film Scheduling,* you will see the making of a movie through the eyes of a production manager. Almost every successful producer or director in Hollywood will tell you that, aside from him- or herself, there is perhaps no one person more important to the successful evolution of a motion picture's schedule than the production manager. He or she is responsible to the director, the producer, the CREW, the ACTORS, the FINANCIERS, the INSURANCE COMPANIES, the COMPLETION BOND COMPANIES, the STUDIO, etc.

A good production manager must be able to find out what makes everyone on the picture tick—from the EXECUTIVE PRODUCER to the GOFER—and find ways for everyone to work together harmoniously (hopefully). Frequently, the production manager is asked to break down the script and prepare the board and budget before the director is hired. The production manager must be able to read the script and make initial decisions from the director's point of view in terms of how a particular scene is going to be shot, how much equipment is going to be needed, etc.

Rarely does an INDEPENDENT PRODUCER have enough money beforehand to hire a production manager to break down the script and prepare a board and budget. Instead, what usually occurs is the producer takes a haphazard guess at what the final figures should be and then calls upon the production manager later on to "fix it." Or, as happens more frequently than not, deals are made by people not experienced in production (although highly qualified in their respective fields) and then the production manager is called upon to produce a "$5 million budget." Why $5 million? Because that's what the deal was made for!

By understanding how to prepare schedules, boards and budgets, the independent producer will not only save time and money by preparing a workable board and budget the first time out, but will also have a better working relationship with the person he chooses as production manager.

There are many different schools of thought on script breakdown and budget preparation—perhaps as many different methods as there are producers in Hollywood with scripts under their arms. What we are presenting here is our method. It works for us, and hopefully, it will work for you.

As we mentioned before, the best way to learn how to schedule and budget is to do it. For those of you who want to participate, the complete script of THE CONVERSATION and all the necessary production forms and sample budget forms are in *The Film Scheduling/Film Budgeting Workbook.* To assist you in understanding all the terminology that you will find in motion picture production, we created *The Filmmakers' Dictionary* of over 1,000 film terms.

We hope that you find these books which comprise *Filmmakers' Library* to be excellent references throughout your filmmaking career. GOOD LUCK and ENJOY!

II

BASIC RULES

Before we begin, here are three basic rules. They are common sense, but should never be forgotten.

Rule Number One: **IF IN DOUBT—ASK!**

Sounds simple enough. Any idiot would, right? Wrong. In pre-production, the only stupid question is the one you forgot to ask. Take for example, the surprised (and embarrassed) LO-CATION MANAGER who forgot to ask whether the lights on the Lincoln Memorial and Washington Monument were on pre-set timers. While filming a feature directed by Sydney Pollack, the full company of over one hundred cast and crew were caught in a dilemma on a Friday night as the lights on the statues started to go out. With the quick assistance of the Washington, D.C. Parks Commission Police and the fast work of a GAFFER who was able to by-pass the switching boxes on the statues' lights, this little neglected question could have turned into a $100,000 disaster.

But, you say, *the mistake was the location manager's—not the production manager's.* Literally, you are right. However, on a production, the production manager is responsible for everything, and ultimately the blame will rest on his shoulders for not having asked the location manager if he checked about the lights. So, to help avoid future situations such as this, ASK QUESTIONS!!!

Rule Number Two: **NEVER ASSUME ANYTHING**

If you *assume* anything on a motion picture project, you will most likely end up making an *ass* out of *u* and *me*. In the example listed in Rule Number One, the location manager *assumed* that the lights on the statues stayed on all the time, the production manager *assumed* that the location manager had taken care of checking about the lights, and the director *assumed* that everything was under control. Luckily, for the production it all worked out. It could have ended up being a really expensive mess.

Rule Number Three: **ALWAYS C. Y. A.***

Make lists. Be organized. Check, double-check and triple check everything. By the time your project is ready to begin, you will know it better than anyone on the payroll. You will have analyzed it from every conceivable angle, and, ideally, come up with every imaginable thing that could go wrong and taken steps to prevent it from happening. In reality, all you will have done is reduce the number of problems which will occur.

As we said in the Chapter One, we are just as anxious as you are to enlist the aid of a computer in keeping track of all the details and are working to make that day come a little bit sooner. In the meantime, we are still going to have to do things by hand.

---

*Cover Your Ass.

III
THE SCRIPT

Those of you who have chosen to break down THE CONVER-
SATION, please turn to *The Film Scheduling/Film Budgeting
Workbook* and read the script. Those of you who have chosen
to break down your own script, please now read it through
entirely. **Do not attempt to break down a script without first
reading it through at least once!**

This will be the first and only time that you will be able to read
this script as a partial spectator, so enjoy it. Sit back and read
the script as you would a good book. Don't rush it, but don't
start to analyze it. Just become familiar with the story line, the
characters' names, the locales, etc. Those of you using THE
CONVERSATION might wish to remove the script from the
book (the sheets are perforated), three-hole punch it and put it
into a three ring binder. It will make it easier to work on when
you begin breaking down the script.

As a production manager, you will receive scripts to break
down that, literally, come in all shapes and sizes. Is there such
as thing as a STANDARD SCRIPT FORMAT? Yes and No. Yes,
there is a format which we prefer and is preferred by most of
the producers and studios (and which you will see in Example

One which follows). No, for some reason, many, many scripts —especially those written and typed by newer and less experienced writers are typed in different formats. Examples of some of these are also included.

An average feature length film whose running time is between 90 and 100 minutes in length will have a screenplay of about 100 to 120 pages when typed in the format shown in Example One. All your future estimates of how long it will take to film a particular scene will be based on the length of that scene. As we will discuss in a later chapter, the smallest fraction of a screen page is one-eighth. You will start to get a feeling for how long it will take to shoot an eighth of a page. When the script is typed in a different format so that either more information or less information is included in that eighth of a page, it is is easy to see how this will affect your calculations. Here, then, are examples of the same page from THE CONVERSATION typed in different formats.

(see next page)

16   CONTINUED   16

> **HARRY**
> (smiling)
> Since when you supposed to be
> entertained?

> **STANLEY**
> Sometimes it's nice to know what
> they're talking about.

> **HARRY**
> (half to himself)
> I don't care what they're
> talking about. I just want a
> nice fat recording.
> (indicates the headset)
> How you doing?

> **STANLEY**
> We're getting better than 4Ø
> percent.

> **HARRY**
> How about the second position?

> **STANLEY**
> Not so good.

Stanley turns the dial up on the sound recorder, and
for a moment the conversation is doubled up on itself.

                                                      CUT TO:

17   TOP OF THE CITY OF PARIS - DAY   17

THE VIEW PANS from the man under the Eiffel Tower sign,
across the park, to another man operating out of an
open window of an office building. He is operating a
second microphone identical to the first one we saw.
It becomes clear that the young couple are being
tracked from two opposing positions. We HEAR the young
man laughing.

18   VIEW ON THE COUPLE   18

> **MARK**
> Where'd you hear that?

> **ANN**
> (also laughing)
> My secret.

                                                      CUT TO:

Analyzing this format from the top, you will see that we have noted *Continued* at the top of the page next to the scene number to indicate that the scene is continued from the previous page. The scene numbers are listed on both sides of the page at the beginning of the scene. There are no spaces between the names of the characters and their dialogue, but there is one space left between the name of the scene and the first line of description.

(*Continued*) is marked again at the bottom of the page to indicate that the scene continues to the next page, or *Cut To*, if the scene ends. If the dialogue continues to the next page, (*More*) should be typed directly under the dialogue. The page number is marked in the upper right hand corner. There are no periods after scene numbers to differentiate them from page numbers. For those of you who may have to type a script, we have included the proper margin settings. For now, just analyze the visible differences you see among the following examples.

Margin Settings

12	-	Scene Numbers - Left Hand
18	-	CONTINUED, SCENE NAME, left-hand margin.
30	-	Begin dialogue
38	-	Dialogue directions (these can also be centered).
44	-	Character names and (MORE)
61	-	End of dialogue
65	-	(CONTINUED), CUT TO, FADE TO, DISSOLVE TO, etc.
73	-	Scene Numbers - Right Hand
78	-	Page Number

>   **HARRY**
>   (smiling)
>   Since when you supposed to be
>   entertained?

>   **STANLEY**
>   Sometimes it's nice to know what
>   they're talking about.

>   **HARRY**
>   (half to himself)
>   I don't care what they're
>   talking about. I just want a
>   nice fat recording.
>   (indicates the headset)
>   How you doing?

>   **STANLEY**
>   We're getting better than 40
>   percent.

>   **HARRY**
>   How about the second position?

>   **STANLEY**
>   Not so good.

HARRY
(smiling)
Since when you supposed to be
entertained?

STANLEY
Sometimes it's nice to know what
they're talking about.

HARRY
(half to himself)
I don't care what they're
talking about. I just want a
nice fat recording.
(indicates the headset)
How you doing?

STANLEY
We're getting better than 40
percent.

HARRY
How about the second position?

STANLEY
Not so good.

Stanley turns the dial up on the sound recorder, and
for a moment the conversation is doubled up on itself.

TOP OF THE CITY OF PARIS - DAY
THE VIEW PANS from the man under the Eiffel Tower sign,
across the park, to another man operating out of an
open window of an office building. He is operating a
second microphone identical to the first one we saw.
It becomes clear that the young couple are being
tracked from two opposing positions. We HEAR the young
man laughing.
VIEW ON THE COUPLE

MARK
Where'd you hear that?

ANN
(also laughing)
My secret.

19 VIEW ON THE MIME
He laughs, as he does a burlesque of the two of them
walking for an amused crowd.
20 MOVING VIEW OF MARK AND ANN
Ignorant of the Mime, still walking

MARK
How do you feel?

ANN
Oh, you know.

14

Although the two extreme opposite examples in Examples Two and Three may seem to be gravely exaggerated, they are samples of actual formats used today. As you can see by comparing them with Example One—the preferred format—the page count that you will end up with will be seriously affected by the way the script is typed. Obviously an eighth of a page of a script typed in the format shown in Example Two is going to be a lot less material to cover than the eighth of a page in Example Three. The more scripts you break down, the more experience you will garner in gauging scene length and when to make allowances and adjustments. For now, just be aware of the differences.

Color Sequences

When revisions are made to FINAL SCRIPTS it is necessary to differentiate between old pages and new pages. The following color-code system is standard in the industry.

1. White
2. Blue
3. Pink
4. Yellow
5. Green
6. Goldenrod

If the writer or person typing the revisions can put an asterisk (*) in the right-hand margin of the line in which there is a change, it will make your job easier. Dialogue changes won't affect your board, ordinarily, but everything else will and can. You won't have to waste time searching for the change if it has been marked.

IV

THE BREAKDOWN SHEET

Breaking down the script to prepare for the production board is a painstaking task. It is also one of the most important parts of scheduling a film. If you forget something during this step, it will surely come back to haunt you. So, as patronizing as this sounds, find yourself a comfortable, quiet, airy room which has good light and claim it! Make sure you will be able to leave your work undisturbed for the duration of the time you are preparing your breakdown and production strip board. Don't start marking any information on your breakdown sheets until you have completely read the following instructions and information.

Gather your materials together and have them within arm's reach. The materials you will need to begin are:

Breakdown Tools
- colored breakdown sheets. (100 each
    of blue, white, green and yellow.)
- several #2 lead pencils
- a transparent ruler

- six water-based fine-tipped marking
    pens in red, orange, yellow,
    green, blue, violet.
- a three-hole punch

> **Note:** We recommend using WATER-BASED MARKING
> PENS as they do not bleed through the paper. For those
> of you who are going to break down THE CONVER-
> SATION, we recommend that you use colored pen-
> cils or crayons. Most scripts are not printed on both
> sides of the paper, and even the best water-based
> markers have been known to bleed through slightly.
> You won't run into this problem when working on a
> script which is printed on only one side of the paper.

On your next reading of the script, you are going to go through
scene by scene and mark every bit of information relative to a
single scene on the appropriate breakdown sheet. Because motion
pictures are usually shot OUT-OF SEQUENCE (meaning Scene 1 could
be shot on the last day of the schedule and Scene 34 on the first
day), and you will be grouping all the DAY SHOTS in the same
location together and all the NIGHT SHOTS in the same location
together, we have found that it is easier and simpler to *color code*
the breakdown sheets. In this way, later on, you will be able to tell
at a glance whether a scene is an Interior or an Exterior, a Day
scene or a Night scene. Take a look at the sample BREAKDOWN SHEETS
at the end of this chapter. Samples of breakdown sheets are in
The Film Scheduling/Film Budgeting Workbook. Later, when you
start transferring information from the breakdown sheets to
the PRODUCTION STRIPS for the PRODUCTION STRIP BOARD, you
will see that we have used the same colors for the strips as we
have for the breakdown sheets. Although it is a little more
expensive to use color-coded sheets, we feel it is better and more
reliable in the long run. When you have been hired to prepare

a board and budget, you will be under the gun time-wise and will need all the help you can get. Physically having to re-read the breakdown sheets every time you want to know whether a scene is an Interior or not is a waste of valuable time.

The color-code for the breakdown sheets (and production strips) is as follows:

YELLOW	-	Exterior Day
WHITE	-	Interior Day
GREEN	-	Exterior Night
BLUE	-	Interior Night

Three-hole punch your sheets so they may be stored in a three-ring binder. Don't let your sheets flop around loose—they can get lost. As soon as you complete the information on one sheet, put it into the binder. You are going to be creating your all-important production board and shooting schedule from these sheets.

The Breakdown Sheet

1. **Date:**   Put in the date you prepare the breakdown sheets, e.g., March 22, 1984.

2. **Key:**   Reminder of the color-codes for the sheets and strips. The small numbers appearing in the boxes refer to the accounting codes on the budget form. These are not of importance until you begin preparing a budget.

3. **Production Company:**   The name of the production company goes here.

4. **Production Title/Number:**   The name of the show, e.g., THE CONVERSATION, goes here. Production compa-

nies which have more than one project in production/ development usually assign production numbers. If known, put than number in here.

5. **Scene No:** The definition of a scene changes from person to person, but for the production manager, it is a unit of action which takes place in the same location over the same period of time. If either the location or the time period changes, then the scene ends and a new one begins. A corollary to this rule says that if the number of actors/ actresses in a scene changes dramatically either at the beginning or the end of a scene, then perhaps a new scene number should be introduced. Most scenes are easily recognizable because the writer has marked INT. (Interior) or EXT. (Exterior) next to the description of the scene **(Union Square - Day)**. However, many times there are scenes hiding within easily identifiable scenes which should be broken out and counted separately. An example of this is in the Warehouse Party scene when suddenly Harry and Meredith are left alone. Originally, Scenes 173 and 174 were all Scene 173. In analyzing the scene, it became obvious that we didn't need to have all the other actors in the Scene 173 available to work in what is now Scene 174 when we only needed Harry and Meredith. So, we split Scene 173 into two scenes and made the second Scene 174.

Sometimes the converse is true. Oftentimes if the writer of the project is also the director, he will break the scene down into shots. Turn to page one of THE CONVERSA-TION. Strictly speaking, there is only one scene on this page, **Ext. Union Square - Day.** But, either Mr. Coppola or Mr. Clark Paylow, (the production manager of THE CONVERSATION) broke this scene into shots. When

20

this happens, do not combine shots back into scenes. Consider each shot as a separate scene and do a separate breakdown sheet for each. It is always better to be more detailed than less detailed when it comes to breaking down a script.

It is usually a production manager's responsibility to number the scenes. Save the numbering until you are ready to transfer the information onto breakdown sheets. You may find that on subsequent readings, there are scenes which should be separated. When numbering your scenes, always number your screenplay on both sides. It makes identification of the scenes much easier.

Added and Omitted Scenes

Go back to the example of Scene 173 and Scene 174. If you had already numbered your script and then decided to divide Scene 173 into two scenes, instead of re-numbering (and then re-typing) the entire script, simply mark the new scene, *Scene 174A*. Don't forget to adjust the breakdown sheets and create a new one for the new scene. If you OMIT a scene, then mark, *Scene 189 - Omitted* on both sides of the screenplay.

6) **Scene Name:** For Scenes 1 through 8 on page 1 of THE CONVERSATION, the official SCENE NAME is **Union Square/Park.** After reading this script through, we know that the story takes place entirely in San Francisco, California, so there is no need to be any more detailed than Union Square/Park. If we were changing cities or moving to very specific locations within Union Square, then it would be necessary to be much more detailed, such as: **Union Square/Park, San Francisco,** or **Union Square/Park - Northeast Corner.**

7) **Description:** This is a brief description of the main action in the scene. As you are going to have to transfer this information to a very small space on a strip, keep this description as brief, yet as concise as possible. For Scene 1, the description would be, *Street musicians play "Red Red Robin"*.

8) **Breakdown Page Number:** This number should correspond to the scene number unless the script you are breaking down has been numbered previously and there are scenes which have been ADDED (usually noted by a letter following a scene number, e.g. "24A") or DELETED (usually noted, "Scene 23 - Omitted"). Unless you find that scenes numbers have been improperly marked, leave the pre-numbered scenes as is. Make sure that you note on a separate piece of paper the numbers of all added and deleted scenes so that you will be able to double-check later on.

9) **Int. or Ext.:** These are abbreviations for Interior and Exterior. Referring to page 1 of THE CONVERSATION, all the scenes on that page are Exteriors—they take place OUTSIDE. Always write out INT. or EXT., not "I" or "E" in the space provided on the Breakdown Sheets.

10) **Day or Night:** Self-explanatory. Again, make sure that you write out DAY or NIGHT in the space provided. If DAWN or DUSK is specifically mentioned or inferred, then write out DAWN or DUSK instead.

Note: Now that you have determined that Scene 1 is a Day/Exterior, you know that the color of your first breakdown sheet will be YELLOW.

11) **Page Count:** This is an area of controversy among production managers. Traditionally, pages of script have been
broken down into eighths of a page for easy calculation,
although there are some production managers who prefer
to use tenths. We prefer eighths. If your screenplay has
been typed in fairly standard format (see Chapter Three),
then there will be about eight or nine inches of typed copy
per page. An eighth of a page, then, equals approximately
one-inch of typed copy. Anything less than one-inch is
always marked, 1/8. Be on the lookout for extra-long
pages and extra-short pages. Just because the writer/typist
put more copy (or less copy) on a page does not mean that
you should always have eight eighths. Some of your pages
will only be 3/8 long. Others will be over 8/8 (e.g. 1-2/8,
etc.) Some scenes are only 1 line long—they are still
marked as 1/8.

When dividing your script into eighths, use your transparent ruler. It is approximately one-inch wide. Using a pencil, draw a line at the beginning of each scene and at the
end of each scene. Measure the area and determine the
length. A scene 2" long will be 2/8, 3" long - 3/8, etc. Do
not convert your fractions—leave them as eighths. It
makes it easier to add and subtract later on. For scenes
longer than 1 page, mark 1-3/8, not 11/8. Full pages
should be marked as "1", not 8/8. Same reason. Always
circle the number and write it in the right hand margin.

Note: Many of you will be tempted to begin your breakdown by lining the script all the way through and then
going through and breaking out the elements. **Do not do
this. Take each scene one at a time.** You may find that at
first glance what appears to be one scene actually is two
and you will have to re-calculate.

CODE — BREAKDOWN SHEETS/STRIPS

Day Ext. — Yellow
Night Ext. — Green
Day Int. — White
Night Int. — Blue
Numbers refer to
budget categories ②

SCRIPT
BREAKDOWN SHEET

① _____
DATE

③ ④ ⑧

PRODUCTION COMPANY ⑤ | PRODUCTION TITLE/NO. ⑥ | BREAKDOWN PAGE NO. ⑨

SCENE NO. ⑦ | SCENE NAME | INT. OR EXT. ⑩

DESCRIPTION | DAY OR NIGHT ⑪

PAGE COUNT

CAST Red (1301-2-3) ⑫	**STUNTS** Orange (1304) ⑬	**EXTRAS/ATMOSPHERE** Green (1322) ⑮
	EXTRAS/SILENT BITS Yellow (1321) ⑭	
SPECIAL EFFECTS Blue (2300) ⑯	**PROPS** Violet (2500) ⑰	**VEHICLES/ANIMALS** Pink (2600/4500) ⑱
WARDROBE Circle (3400) ⑲	**MAKE-UP/HAIR** Asterisk (3500) ⑳	**SOUND EFFECTS/MUSIC** Brown (5100,5300,5400) ㉑
SPECIAL EQUIPMENT Box ㉒	**PRODUCTION NOTES** ㉓	

© 1984 Lone Eagle Productions, Inc.

The Breakdown Sheet

Marking The Elements On The Script Page

We have completed the description part of the breakdown sheet and have now come to the individual elements: Numbers 12-23 (beginning with CAST). Using the water-based pens (or crayons/colored pencils), we will color-code these elements using a system which we feel makes it much easier and simpler. The best way to mark the elements is to UNDERLINE—not highlight. During the course of the production, this marked and lined script may have to be photocopied. If highlighter pens are used over the typewritten copy, chances are it will be difficult (or sometimes impossible) to read or photocopy. By underlining, not only will you be able to read the words, but you will also be able to use brighter, more easily identifiable colors than you would with highlighters. **Remember: Do not mark anything on your script until you have read this chapter completely** When you start going through each scene to find the elements, the extra step of marking that particular element in a certain color on the script is, in effect, a cross-checking safe-guard. You will 1) read the script, 2) color-code the element on the script, and 3) write down the element on the breakdown sheet. We suggest using a pencil on the breakdown sheets in case you find something you have to change or delete.

The color-coding system is as follows:

Color		Element
RED	-	**CAST - SPEAKING**
ORANGE	-	**STUNTS**
YELLOW	-	**EXTRAS - SILENT BITS**
GREEN	-	**EXTRAS - ATMOSPHERE**

BLUE	-	**SPECIAL EFFECTS**
VIOLET	-	**PROPS**
PINK	-	**VEHICLES/ANIMALS**
BROWN	-	**SOUND EFFECTS**

Circle all the WARDROBE information, mark all MAKE-UP and HAIR information with an Asterisk, and put a box around all SPECIAL EQUIPMENT information. Any other pertinent information should be underlined in black and listed under Production Notes (using a pen, not a marker.)

Inside, each box you will notice three things: 1) the name of the category, such as CAST, 2) the name of a color (*red*) in parentheses to remind you which color you should be using when highlighting or underlining this information, and 3) a number also in parentheses (*1301-2-3*). These numbers correspond to the budget form categories. They are not of importance to you now, but will be in the future when you transfer all this information to the budget form.

Before marking anything, please read through all this information.

12) **Cast - Speaking:** UNDERLINE IN RED any person who utters one single word in the script. They are considered to have a SPEAKING part and must be scheduled and paid according to Screen Actors Guild (SAG) rules. PRINCIPALS are the leads in the film (Harry Caul, Ann and Mark would be Principals). SUPPORTING PLAYERS are the actors who have large parts, but are not the leads. (Stanley, Paul, Martin, etc., are Supporting Players.) DAY PLAYERS are actors who have only a few lines or a few scenes. (e.g., the people who live in Harry's apartment building are Day Players. So are Tony, Harry's niece, and

McNaught, Harry's attorney.) This information will be important later on when you begin to lay out your schedule and also when you do your budget. But for now, you will list all SPEAKING PARTS together here in the same category.

When you begin marking your script, UNDERLINE the character's name (or any element which you are marking) the first time it appears on the page, and then again on every succeeding page. If it is not mentioned again on the next page, but it is implied, write it in the margin and mark it with the appropriate color highlighter.

The first time a speaking part is mentioned in a scene, mark the character's full name in capitals (e.g., *HARRY CAUL*) on the breakdown sheet. Every time thereafter, you can use his first and/or last name, but it should be written in lower case (e.g., *Harry* or *Harry Caul*) By doing this, you will be able to tell later on when all your breakdown sheets have been re-shuffled that you have not missed any of the characters, and in which scene an actor first appears in the script.

If the actor in your script is a child, note the age the child is to play and list a WELFARE WORKER/TEACHER under production notes.

13) **Stunts:** UNDERLINE IN ORANGE. Any hazardous, or potentially hazardous, act or action which will be performed by a specially-trained person instead of the main actor is a stunt. If you find when reading through your script that there seems to be a fair amount of stunt work, then you will probably need a STUNT COORDINATOR in addition to the STUNT DOUBLES. Mark STUNT COORDI-

NATOR under **PRODUCTION NOTES** for the corresponding scene and the name of the **CHARACTER** and **STUNT DOUBLE** under **CAST MEMBER**.

In Scene 365, we see Mr. C. in his wrecked Mercedes Benz slumped over the steering wheel. In the next second, the car bursts into flames. Depending on how close the director wants to get, we may either use a Stunt Double or a **DUMMY** which would be made by **SPECIAL EFFECTS**. Make sure that you mark both possibilities under Production Notes and *Mr. C.* and *Mr. C - Stunt Double* under *Cast - Speaking.* It may also be necessary for the actor playing Mr. C. to be there for **CLOSE-UPS**. In THE CONVERSATION, the actor (Robert Duvall) was required to be present.

14) **Extras - Silent Bits:**   UNDERLINE IN YELLOW any actor who, under direction, performs an action or causes an action to be performed in a scene which then becomes part of the story line.

Referring to Scene 17, the MAN ON THE EIFFEL TOWER with the shotgun microphone who tracks Ann and Mark as they make their way through Union Square Park is a **SILENT**. Silents or **SILENT BITS** are **EXTRAS** who have been **UP-GRADED** to a higher pay scale, but not as high as **DAY PLAYER**.

Refer now to Scene 3 where the Young Mime is dressed as a Drum Major. We have a tricky problem here—is this character a Silent? or a Speaking Part? By nature, mimes are silent. You could carry this logic to an extreme and say that if you were to do a film with Marcel Marceau he would be a Silent. Common sense has to prevail, though and tell you that if Marceau were one of the leads in the film, he would be listed as a "Principal" and therefore "Speaking" part. In this scene, however, the Young Mime imitates a man carrying a cup of hot coffee. The "man" turns out to be Harry Caul. Because in this scene, the Mime interacts with the main character and, in fact, *talks* to the surrounding crowd, we have listed the Mime as a speaking part and underlined his character in red. An equally logical case can be built for listing the Mime as a Silent. When you get into budgeting, you'll see that the rate for a "Speaking" actor is much higher than for a "Silent." We prefer to err on the high side.

15) **Extras - Atmosphere:** UNDERLINE IN GREEN. Atmosphere actors (aka Extras) are the actors who fill in the background and make the film look real. In the opening scenes of THE CONVERSATION (Specifically Scenes 1 and 2) the band which sets up and then later plays is listed as "Silent." But the "crowds of shoppers . . . and office workers out for their lunch hour" are listed as "Atmospheres." In this space on the breakdown sheet, you are going to make a rough estimate of how many people you are going to need and of what type (*how many office workers? how many shoppers?*). Your ability to guess accurately will improve with experience.

Screen Actors Guild vs. Screen Extras Guild

On the West Coast, all EXTRAS—Silents and Atmospheres —are under the jurisdiction of the Screen Extras Guild (SEG). There are very specific categories of EXTRAS with corresponding pay scales. In New York and Chicago, these separate categories exist, but all actors (including "Extras") are under the jurisdiction of the Screen Actors Guild (SAG). It is best to consult your local Screen Actors Guild and Screen Extras Guild.

16) **Special Effects:** UNDERLINE IN BLUE. To most people, Special Effects means only what they saw in RAIDERS OF THE LOST ARK, STAR WARS and ET. Special Effects means, literally, any effect which is special and which must be created. A working kitchen sink may not be *special* to you, but in movie terminology it is called a PRACTICAL SINK and falls under the category of SPECIAL EFFECTS. All the elements—fire, air and water—in all their various forms (rain, mud, hurricanes, floods, fires, etc.) and their resulting damage (exploding buildings, mountains caving in, avalanches, etc.) are all SPECIAL EFFECTS.

In Scene 43, "Harry cooks two porkchops." If this scene were shot in an actual apartment with a kitchenette, chances are that the stove would work. If this scene were shot on a stage, however, then a practical stove would have to be set up—SPECIAL EFFECTS DEPARTMENT.

17) **Props:** UNDERLINE IN VIOLET. Any portable object which is used in a scene by one of the actors is considered to be a PROP ("property") and comes under the jurisdiction of the PROP DEPARTMENT. If the object is part of the decor of the set, then it is considered SET DRESSING. As a particular prop may have to be made (or bought) in duplicate or triplicate, it is very important to list every single prop on the appropriate breakdown sheet.

Deciding where a prop is necessary may sometimes take some reading between the lines on your part. Re-read scenes 188 through 221. We FADE IN on Golden Gate Park where Harry confronts Stanley, CUT TO Harry walking to the Financial Plaza and into the elevator, and finally up to meet Mr. C. and Martin. In Scene 188, the easel with a large number 7 should be listed as a Prop. In Scene 189, Harry is carrying a blue plastic pouch which should be listed on Breakdown Sheet No. 189. As we know from reading the script, that blue plastic pouch contains the tape recording which Harry made of Ann and Mark. The pouch is not mentioned again until Scene 199, page 94, when he is inside the elevator. Although it is not specifically mentioned, it is possible that the blue plastic pouch could be seen in every single scene from 189 through 199. Therefore, you will need to mark, *blue plastic pouch* on those corresponding breakdown sheets.

18) **Vehicles & Animals:**   UNDERLINE IN PINK. VEHICLES used to refer only to PICTURE CARS. We have expanded the category to refer to all vehicles which will be necessary in the scene. PICTURE CARS are vehicles used by the PRINCIPAL ACTORS in a scene, or which play a major part in the action of the scene. ATMOSPHERE VEHICLES are all other vehicles which are seen on the screen.

Refer to Scene 143 where Harry and group are in the parking lot of the St. Francis Hotel. PAUL'S STAFF CAR is a PICTURE CAR. The rest of the parked cars in the lot as well as the "city traffic" which Paul pulls out into and joins are ATMOSPHERE CARS.

Note the number of PICTURE CARS and ATMOSPHERE VEHICLES which you will need in each scene. Again, you are going to have to use your imagination. If the director is going to shoot this from a HIGH, WIDE ANGLE where you will see a lot of cars in the parking lot and on the street, you will need more than if he stays in very CLOSE. This is a question which only your director can answer, so make a note of it. When you mark, "Paul's Staff Car" make sure you also describe it (a grey sedan with a code number on the side). Later on in Scene 155 you will notice in the screen directions that a "mobile telephone receiver" is mentioned. Make sure that you go back to Breakdown Sheet No. 143 (and wherever else Paul's Staff Car is mentioned) and make a note of it. Most likely, a special antenna will have to be added to the hood of the car. Also, remind yourself to check and see if there is a special license plate which a staff car should carry. Your ART DEPARTMENT will need to know this.

ANIMALS in a scene require special handling. For each animal, or group of animals (such as horses, cows, sheep, etc.) you are going to need a TRAINER/HANDLER or WRANGLER. If the animal is required to perform special tricks or actions, then a specially-trained animal and trainer will be required. Many times, as in the case of Benji (or Lassie), there was not just one particular dog, but rather a group of look-alike dogs—each of which had been taught to do a specific action or trick.

In Scenes 202, 204 and 205, a large, black, Doberman Pinscher—obviously a trained attack dog—appears at the corridor. Mark the description of the dog under Vehicles and Animals and Handler—Attack Dog under Production Notes. As the dog appears quite calm in this scene, it may not be necessary to have a full-fledged attack-trained dog. Maybe just a trained Doberman will suffice. Make a note and ask the director.

19) **Wardrobe:** Put a **CIRCLE** around any piece of wardrobe information described in the script and list it here. Most often, the wardrobe worn by the principal players will have to be available in duplicate or triplicate. In

scenes where the wardrobe is intentionally ripped or soiled, it is not uncommon to have a dozen or more copies of wardrobe available for RE-TAKES

20) **Make-Up and Hair:** Mark all make-up and hair references with an ASTERISK and list here. These notations will be especially important if the project is a PERIOD PIECE as more time will have to be allowed to prepare the actors before going on the set.

21) **Sound Effects & Music:** UNDERLINE IN BROWN. Any sound which must be recorded or pre-recorded should be listed here. Birds chirping, applause, or, as you see in Scene 1, the song—*Red, Red, Robin*. When a song such as that is needed in a particular scene, make a note under Production Notes that you will have to obtain (and pay for) the rights to use this song.

THE CONVERSATION poses a particular problem with regard to Sound Effects as a large portion of the screenplay refers to pre-recorded dialogue. When we go through the schedule, you will see what we mean. For now, just note and be aware of scenes which will involve playback of an original recording.

22) **Special Equipment:** BOXED IN BLACK. Unless specifically noted in a scene, you will have to use your imagination and common sense to mark any necessary equipment in this category. Again, you will have a lot of questions to ask the Director. If the scene says, ZOOM IN then you will require a special ZOOM LENS. If the scene says, SLOW MOTION, then you will need a VARIABLE SPEED MOTOR which will allow you to film at a rate faster than the normal 24 frames per second. If it seems

33

that the shot is going to be taken from a helicopter, then you should note that you will need a special HELICOPTER WITH A CAMERA MOUNT and perhaps another CAMERA OPERATOR who has been trained in helicopter work.

Referring again to Scene 143 in the *Parking Lot - Hotel St. Francis,* you may find out that the director would like to shoot this from a high, wide angle, necessitating a CRANE. Or, perhaps the director would like to follow along with the car as it drives out of the Parking Lot. This could be accomplished by using either a DOLLY or a CAMERA MOUNT on a CAMERA CAR, the latter could follow the car into traffic and stay with it.

In THE CONVERSATION, you will see that special SURVEILLANCE EQUIPMENT is needed. Mark SURVEILLANCE EQUIPMENT under Props, and also under Special Equipment. As soon as we have more details, we will include them. Note that you will need a TECHNICAL ADVISOR for all this surveillance equipment to ensure the accuracy in the film. Don't get lazy and mark it just once —mark SURVEILLANCE EQUIPMENT under Special Equipment and TECHNICAL ADVISOR under Production Notes (See 23) every time they are mentioned or inferred in the script.

23) **Production Notes:** UNDERLINED IN BLACK (pen—not marker.) Throughout this chapter, we have mentioned things which should be included under Production Notes: Wardrobe, Technical Advisors, Animal Handlers, Welfare Worker for Child Actors, etc. List all your questions about a particular scene in this area as well as anything which you need to clarify with the director.

You will create your **SHOOTING SCHEDULE** and your **PRO-DUCTION BOARD** from these **BREAKDOWN SHEETS**. Although not a great deal of information can fit onto a strip, the Shooting Schedule should and does contain all the pertinent facts. Be detailed and be accurate.

Before you begin your breakdown of THE CONVERSATION; read over the following scenes and the corresponding breakdown sheets which we have as examples.

Her big eyes follow at the spot where he stood for a
while, and then she lies back down on the bed.

                                                    CUT TO:

48   INT. HARRY'S SMALL LIVING ROOM - NIGHT   48

The single room is dominated by a large homemade
loudspeaker, a single speaker as in the old Hi Fi days.
We HEAR a Jazz record, old, but well-preserved.

THE VIEW ALTERS and reveals Harry seated on a
straight-back wooden chair in the center of his Living
Room, holding a saxophone, and furiously playing along
with the recording.

The sax solo finishes, to great applause from the live
audience, and a sweating, winded Harry closes his eyes
and takes it for himself.

                                                    FADE OUT:

FADE IN:

49   EXT. HARRY'S BUILDING - DAY   49

A construction crew has begun work on the demolition of
an abandoned row of Victorian buildings. We HEAR
sounds of trucks and hammers. Harry exits the
building, passes the construction work and sits and
waits at the stop for the electric bus.

                                                    CUT TO:

50   EXT. WAREHOUSE AREA - DAY   50

Harry walks parallel to some railroad tracks in the
industrial part of the city. Trucks double park, and
there is loading and unloading in progress. Perhaps a
train goes by.

Harry steps into the warehouse building, pushes a
button, and rises up into the building.

                                                    CUT TO:

51   INT. HARRY'S WAREHOUSE OFFICE - DAY   51

Harry rises in an industrial elevator up into the
warehouse area. We notice benches with electronic
equipment, some cabinets and shelves, a screened-off
area. Stanley is lounging around on an old sofa
reading a magazine.

                                        (CONTINUED)

The Breakdown Sheet

SCRIPT
BREAKDOWN SHEET

DATE _MARCH 22, 1984_

BREAKDOWN PAGE NO. _48_

PRODUCTION COMPANY _48_	PRODUCTION TITLE/NO. _HARRY'S APT. BLDG/H's LIVINGROOM_	BREAKDOWN PAGE NO.
SCENE NO.	SCENE NAME	INT. OR EXT. _INT_

DESCRIPTION _HARRY PLAYS SAX SOLO w/RECORD_

DAY OR NIGHT _NIGHT_

PAGE COUNT _3/8_

CAST Red (1301-2-3)	STUNTS Orange (1304)	EXTRAS/ATMOSPHERE Green (1322)
HARRY		
	EXTRAS/SILENT BITS Yellow (1321)	

SPECIAL EFFECTS Blue (2300)	PROPS Violet (2500)	VEHICLES/ANIMALS Pink (2600/4500)
	-1 LARGE HOMEMADE LOUDSPEAKER (OLD-FASHIONED) ALTEC A-500 _- STRAIGHT-BACK WOODEN CHAIR_ _- SAXOPHONE_	

WARDROBE Circle (3400)	MAKE-UP/HAIR Asterisk (3500)	SOUND EFFECTS/MUSIC Brown (5100,5300,5400)
		JAZZ RECORD w/APPLAUSE

SPECIAL EQUIPMENT Box	PRODUCTION NOTES
	- TECH ADVISOR-SAX _- MAKE-UP, HARRY SWEATING_

CODE — BREAKDOWN SHEETS/STRIPS
Day Ext. — Yellow
Night Ext. — Green
Day Int. — White
Night Int. — Blue
Numbers refer to
budget categories

SCRIPT
BREAKDOWN SHEET

MARCH 22, 1984
DATE

49
BREAKDOWN PAGE NO.

PRODUCTION COMPANY	PRODUCTION TITLE/NO.	
49	HARRY'S APT. BLDG	EXT.
SCENE NO.	SCENE NAME	INT. OR EXT.
HARRY EXITS BLDG + PASSES DEMOLITION CREW		DAY
DESCRIPTION		DAY OR NIGHT
		2/8
		PAGE COUNT

CAST Red (1301-2-3) HARRY	STUNTS Orange (1304)	EXTRAS/ATMOSPHERE Green (1322) CONSTRUCTION CREW (25) 15 N.D. EXTRAS
	EXTRAS/SILENT BITS Yellow (1321)	
SPECIAL EFFECTS Blue (2300)	PROPS Violet (2500) BUS STOP SIGN BENCH	VEHICLES/ANIMALS Pink (2600/4500)
WARDROBE Circle (3400)	MAKE-UP/HAIR Asterisk (3500)	SOUND EFFECTS/MUSIC Brown (5100,5300,5400) DEMOLITION SOUNDS
SPECIAL EQUIPMENT Box BUILDING/CONSTRUCTION CREW - TRUCKS, JACK HAMMERS, CRANE ?	PRODUCTION NOTES	

© 1984 Lone Eagle Productions, Inc.

CODE — BREAKDOWN SHEETS/STRIPS
Day Ext. — Yellow
Night Ext. — Green
Day Int. — White
Night Int. — Blue
Numbers refer to
budget categories

SCRIPT
BREAKDOWN SHEET

MARCH 22, 1984
DATE

_50_
BREAKDOWN PAGE NO.

PRODUCTION COMPANY	PRODUCTION TITLE/NO.	
_50_	_INDUSTRIAL AREA/HARRY'S WHSE._	_EXT_
SCENE NO.	SCENE NAME	INT. OR EXT.

HARRY ENTERS WAREHOUSE ELEVATOR
DESCRIPTION

DAY
DAY OR NIGHT

_2/8_
PAGE COUNT

CAST Red (1301-2-3) _HARRY_	STUNTS Orange (1304)	EXTRAS/ATMOSPHERE Green (1322) _25 WAREHOUSE TYPES_
	EXTRAS/SILENT BITS Yellow (1321)	
SPECIAL EFFECTS Blue (2300)	PROPS Violet (2500) _ASSORTED BOXES_	VEHICLES/ANIMALS Pink (2600/4500) _TRUCKS (DOUBLE PARKED)_
WARDROBE Circle (3400)	MAKE-UP/HAIR Asterisk (3500)	SOUND EFFECTS/MUSIC Brown (5100,5300,5400)
SPECIAL EQUIPMENT Box _FREIGHT TRAIN, FORK LIFTS, HAND TRUCKS, ETC. INDUSTRIAL ELEVATOR OR ELEVATOR IN WAREHOUSE W/ BUTTON_	PRODUCTION NOTES _TECHNICAL ADVISOR- INDUSTRIAL ELEVATOR_	

| CODE — BREAKDOWN SHEETS/STRIPS
Day Ext. — Yellow
Night Ext. — Green
Day Int. — White
Night Int. — Blue
Numbers refer to
budget categories | **SCRIPT
BREAKDOWN SHEET** | *MARCH 22, 1984*
DATE |

		51 BREAKDOWN PAGE NO.
PRODUCTION COMPANY	PRODUCTION TITLE/NO.	
51	*HARRY'S WAREHOUSE - OFFICE*	*INT.*
SCENE NO.	SCENE NAME	INT. OR EXT.
HARRY + STANLEY TALK		*DAY*
DESCRIPTION		DAY OR NIGHT
		6/8
		PAGE COUNT

CAST Red (1301-2-3) *HARRY* *STANLEY*	**STUNTS** Orange (1304)	**EXTRAS/ATMOSPHERE** Green (1322)
	EXTRAS/SILENT BITS Yellow (1321)	
SPECIAL EFFECTS Blue (2300)	**PROPS** Violet (2500) *BENCHES* *ELECTRONIC SURVEILLANCE* * EQUIPMENT* *CABINETS + SHELVES* *OLD SOFA* *MAGAZINE* *THREE PROF. TAPE RECORDERS* *MANILA ENVELOPE - SEVERAL PHOTOS*	**VEHICLES/ANIMALS** Pink (2600/4500)
WARDROBE Circle (3400)	**MAKE-UP/HAIR** Asterisk (3500)	**SOUND EFFECTS/MUSIC** Brown (5100,5300,5400)
SPECIAL EQUIPMENT Box	**PRODUCTION NOTES** *1. TECH. ADVISOR - SURVEILLANCE EQUIP.* *2. COAT/ HARRY* *3. SEVERAL PHOTOS OF ANN + MARK* * 8 X 10 B+W TAKEN FROM SURVEILLANCE SCENE. IF* * SHOT FIRST — OTHERWISE MUST BE STAGED* * (SCHEDULE STILL SESSION)*	

V

THE PRODUCTION BOARD

Now that you have completed your breakdown sheets, we can move on to the next step:

Creating the Production Board

In order to schedule your film project, you must be able to look at all the variables and re-arrange their order easily. You will need to do this not only at the beginning of your project when you are estimating length and cost, but also during the actual shooting of the project. As you will see in later chapters, it is not unusual for a schedule to be re-arranged during shooting to accommodate a change. These changes come from your **PARAMETER GUIDES** (see Chapter VI). If you were trying to schedule your project using only the breakdown sheets, you would have quite a cumbersome task in trying to look at all the sheets simultaneously. To facilitate scheduling, only the most pertinent information is listed on a small, color-coded **PRODUCTION STRIP** which is stored on the **PRODUCTION BOARD**. This board can be handled and transported easily, and can be almost any length you wish. Commercially produced strips and strip boards are either 15" high or 18-1/4" high. We recommend that you use the 15" strips and board as they can easily be photocopied. The 18-1/4" strips are too long and photocopying would require too much cutting and pasting. When you choose which height board you are going to work with, try to purchase all the strips from one manufacturer. Although they are all basically the same, the lines on the strips do vary from manufacturer to manufacturer and if you mix them, they won't line up.

Production boards are constructed from different materials— cardboard or wood are the usual choices. Cardboard boards are the least expensive and most commonly used. Both the cardboard and wooden boards come in varying sizes according to the number of PANELS. One panel holds approximately 25 strips and is about 10 inches wide. The average feature film project would require a board approximately 6 to 8 panels in length. THE CONVERSATION will require at least 8 panels.

If you find that you are going to be using a Strip Board on a fairly regular basis, it might be advisable to have one built (or build it yourself). It will cost from $100 on up depending on how many panels, what materials you use and how elaborate you want to get. At this writing, an eight-panel cardboard board now costs about $85, so you might want to consider acquiring your own board sooner than later. If you do decide to have one made, make sure that the working surface (the area where you will place your strips) is slightly convex. Your strips will stay in place much better than in the standard flat surface board because of the slight tension placed on them due to the design. Dependable hinges and a good leather carrying handle are also good ideas.

You will be able to buy strips and boards from the following companies:

Gilbert Mandelik (handcrafted wood boards only)
1650 N. Kings Road
Los Angeles, CA 90069
213/654-5524

Peter Griffin
Hollywood Production Boards
7469 Melrose Avenue #29
Los Angeles, CA 90046
213/651-4220

Production Boards by Jack Cash
650 N. Bronson
Los Angeles, CA 90004
213/463-5885

Enterprise Stationers
7401 Sunset Blvd.
Los Angeles, CA 90046
213/876-3530

Earl Hays Press
10707 Sherman Way
Sun Valley, CA 91352
213/765-0700

F & B Ceco
315 West 43rd Street
New York, New York 10036
212/974-4600

Materials

1 bundle of each of the following color strips: blue, green, white, yellow, fluorescent pink, and either red or orange.

1 bundle strips which are white at the top and black on the bottom.

2 Headers (Head Boards).

2 or 3 black pens which will not smear. Ball points work very well as do "Penstix" (Alvin - EEF). You can find these at good art supply stores. Their ink is very good (also indelible) and reproduces well on copy machines. We do not recommend using regular felt tips as they tend to smear.

Bottles of "white-out" fluid in colors to match the strips.

1 Production Strip Board - about 8 panels.

1 two-panel Strip Board which will serve as your Holding Board.

Several different colors of small adhesive "dots"—suggest red, black, green, etc. These could be used to mark scenes which take place in another city, or in the case of THE CONVERSA-TION, we will use them to mark the scenes in which the dialogue has been pre-recorded.

Head Board

To begin making your Production Board, start with the Head Board or Header. Refer to the example in this chapter. The Header will be the index for all the other information which you will put on the strips to eventually make your Production Board. Since every manufacturer of strips and head has its own particular listing of information, you may find that you will have to re-arrange the order to suit your needs.

Your Head Board lines should read as follows:

> **Line 1** - Blank, in case you need to mark anything extraordinary such as Second Unit, Change in Time Period, Material to be shot in another country/state/city, etc. This is a good place for the "dots" which we mentioned earlier.
>
> **Line 2** - Day or Night
>
> **Line 3** - Breakdown Page Number
>
> **Line 4** - Exterior or Interior
>
> **Line 5** - Scene Number

Go on down the strip and fill in the appropriate information next to, **Title, Director, Producer, Assistant Director,** etc. Fill in **Prod. Mgr.** and the appropriate name in the space which follows.

Another important step is to find a place on your headboard and write the date the script was written. Usually, you will find the date on the title page of the script. If there is none, write in the date on which you complete the production board. It is very likely that the script will undergo some rewrites which may necessitate changing the board. Dating the board and the script will make it easier to identify later on. Mark the date only on the header—not on the individual strips themselves.

The next group of lines is reserved for the cast members. Go back to your breakdown sheets and, on a separate piece of paper entitled **Cast,** list each character and the number of the scene in which the actor appears. Don't just make a "tick" mark, list the actual scene number. You will need this information later on. List every actor/actress who says one word (including voice-overs), and then count the total number of scenes for each character. The actor/actress who has the most number of scenes is #1, the actor/actress with the second number of scenes is #2, and so forth. The only time you will make an exception is out of respect to a well-known actor who may have a smaller part. In THE CONVERSATION, Harry Caul is #1, Ann is #2, Mark is #3, and Mr. C is #4. You know that Mr. C has fewer scenes than either Stanley or Paul, but yet he is listed in fourth position. Well, when THE CONVERSATION was made, Robert Duvall, who played Mr. C, was much more well-known than John Cazale who played Stanley, and Michael Higgins who played Paul. Again, if you have a hesitation about which actor should be listed first, it is a good idea to check with the producer (or director) so that there aren't any unintentional slights.

If you find that you have more than 25 speaking parts, you have a choice—either double them up or use a separate head board. In the case of THE CONVERSATION, we chose to double up as the smaller speaking parts were not all in the same scenes. Don't list the actor/actress' names, as that can change. List only the name of the character.

Note: Never use the bottom ten spaces of the Head Board for Characters' names — this will be explained later.

Since we have more than 25 speaking parts, we have listed only seventeen of the most important and then split the column in two. Take the time to white out the numbers which you will not need and to write in the correct number—now. Once a number is assigned to a character, that is his/her number throughout the entire production board and later on in the shooting schedule. Some production managers alternate red and black ink so that they will stand out. Other production managers list the minor characters' names in a different color ink and then double them up all the way on the board. We prefer not to rely on different color inks as you won't be able to differentiate them when they are photocopied (unless it's a color copier). If you find that you are going to be working on a very long project—a mini-series, for example, then we urge you to use as many head boards as you need. Fill in only the **Character** section of the head board, and place it to the right of the main head board.

In the bottom ten spaces, we shall list other elements which will be specially scheduled. Some of these and their corresponding code letters are:

Music	(M)
Special Effects	(SFX)
Special Equipment	(SE)
Animals	(A)
Extras (*actual number*)	(#)
Rain	(R)

You will find that you will develop your own symbols for these. There are others which you will think of. Establish your own system and legend. Always put a circle around these elements to help draw your attention to them. In the case of Extras, it is essential that you circle the number as you may become confused with the character number.

Filling in the Strips

When beginning to fill in the strips, it is wise to use your two-panel Holding Board. You can also use a large flat table, but chances are your strips will get out of order and everything won't be lined up properly. Finish all the strips for one sequence before transferring them over to your large board. Keep your strips in chronological order—don't try to jump ahead.

Day or Nite		
BREAK DOWN PAGE #		
EXTERIOR OR INTERIOR		
SCENE #		
Title THE CONVERSATION		
Director FRANCIS COPPOLA		
Producer		
Asst. Director		
PROD'N MGR CLARK PAYLOW		
NO. OF PAGES		

Character	Artist	No.
HARRY CAUL		1
ANN		2
MARK		3
MR. C.		4
STANLEY		5
PAUL MEYERS		6
MARTIN		7
WILLIAM P. MORGAN		8
MEREDITH		9
MILLARD		10
MRS. GOETNER		11
RON KELLER		12
MRS. CORSITTO		13
BOB		14
BOB'S WIFE		15
AMY		16
LURLEEN		17
MALE SEC'Y 18	TONY	19
MALE RECEPT. 20	MIME	21
YOUNG MAN 22	YOUNG WOMAN	23
SHOPPER #1 24	SHOPPER #2	25
SHOPPER #3 26	LAUNDRY LADY	27
#27'S Little Boy 28	WOMAN #1-ELEV	29
WOMAN #2-ELEV. 30	MAN IN ELEVATOR	31
DEMO MAN 32	SPEAKER	33
MAN IN BOOTH 34	YOUNG DRIVER	35
MOTEL CLERK 36	BUS DRIVER #1	37
BUS DRIVER #2 38	MCNAUGHT	39
ANNC'R/PA SYST. 40	TEL. OPER #1	41
CHROME DOME UO 42	WOMAN IN RRm	43
TEL. OPER. #2 44	MAN #2 IN BOOTH	45
MUSIC : Ⓜ	CARS : Ⓒ	
SPECIAL EQUIPMENT : ⑥Ⓔ		
ANIMALS : A		
EXTRAS: Ⓕ		

Your project may not have as many scenes (or shots) as THE CONVERSATION has. One hundred fifty to two hundred scenes would be considered fairly normal for a 100 - 120 page script. Usually, we recommend that you put each scene on a separate strip. In the case of THE CONVERSATION, however, we are dealing with over 300 scenes, many of which are just different angles of the same scene. In this case it is perfectly alright to combine scenes onto one strip, so long as all the information is exactly the same and represents only a change in angle. If you are at all hesitant, then put the information on separate strips. Be aware that if you do combine shots onto one strip, you may have to go back later and make individual strips if something changes in a revision.

Now you can begin making your strips. As mentioned earlier, the production strips are also color-coded to correspond to the breakdown sheets: YELLOW = Day Exterior, WHITE = Day Interior, GREEN = Night Exterior, BLUE = Night Interior. Look at your first breakdown sheet—Yellow, which tells you the shot is a Day Exterior. Take your yellow strip and place it in the holding board to the right of the head board, making sure that the lines line up evenly. Don't start writing yet.

Now, look back at your breakdown sheets. Scenes 1 - 11 all take place in Union Square, so perhaps they could all be listed on one strip. Looking a little closer, we see that Scenes 10 and 11 are views from the rooftop overlooking the Square, so let's break them out. Look at the rest of the Scenes 1 - 9. Go back and re-read the scenes in the script. We don't discover Harry Caul until Scene 3 and don't meet Ann and Mark until Scene 9. From the way it is written, however, it is very possible that all three of these characters could be seen in the background and just not identified until later scenes. As the location, time of day, number of extras, etc., are all the same, we have chosen to combine Scenes 1 - 9 onto one strip. When you do this, make sure that you go through all the corresponding breakdown sheets and transfer all the pertinent information from each sheet onto the strip.

Beginning at the top of the strip, these scenes take place in the daytime, so, if it isn't already pre-printed on your yellow strip, mark "D." These are breakdown sheets 1-9 and they are an EXT. The scenes are 1-9. In the space corresponding to the space marked Script Dated on the head board, mark the PAGE COUNT. Go through the first nine breakdown sheets and total the number of pages you have. It should be 3-3/8. (If you are not sure, go back to your script to double-check.)

Then go through and fill in the characters which appear. Whenever a character appears in a scene (or group of shots) mark the number of the character (e.g., #2 for Ann) in the corresponding space. Do not just mark an "X" or "√."

In the event that two characters who are sharing the same space have to appear in the same scene, just move one of the characters up or down one space or divide the space with a slash (/). This probably won't happen too often.

Now, go through the first nine breakdown sheets and mark every character who appears in any of the nine scenes. Your strip will have the following marked on it: #1—Harry Caul, #2—Ann, #3—Mark, #21—Mime, #22—Young Man, #23—Young Woman, M—Music, SE—Special Equipment and 125—Extras. When you have completed all the information to be listed across the strip horizontally, turn your board one-quarter turn sideways. In the blank space at the top of the strip between "Scene #" and "Page Count" write out the location of the scene, e.g., **Union Square**. In the space at the very bottom of the strip, write out a brief description of the action. You will get this information from the breakdown sheets. Don't use full sentences. The shorter the better. *"Surveillance"* is how we describe these scenes.

Now that you understand how to complete your first strip, fill it in and leave it in the holding board. Proceed with the next strip, following the same steps which we outlined above.

From time to time, you will see that an actor/actress is mentioned in one scene and it is implied that he/she should be in the next scene. If you are unclear as to whether the actor/actress should be in the scene and you haven't been able to ask the director, mark the actor/actress as appearing in the scene and put a question mark beside the number. Two good examples of this are Scene 34 - Exterior Bus, and Scene 35 - Interior Bus. In Scene 34, Harry is not mentioned, but he appears in Scene 35. We will put a "?" beside his number (#1) in Scene 34, as we are not sure whether he will be seen by the camera or not. Mark this, and any other questions you will have, on your list of questions to ask the director and/or producer.

THE CONVERSATION uses footage more than one time. This doesn't mean that you have to shoot it more than once, only that it has to be scheduled and accounted for. In order to differentiate between previously shot material and new material, we have put a small horizontal line in the top-most square of the appropriate strip. We could also use small dots, or any other mark which you prefer which is clear, distinct and uniform.

Even though you have gone through the breakdown sheets, it is a good idea to have your marked-up script handy so that you

Title: **THE CONVERSATION**
Director: **FRANCIS COPPOLA**
Producer:
Asst. Director:
Prod'n Mgr: **CLARK PAYLOW**

Day or Nite	D	D	D	D	D	D	D	D	D	D	D	D	D	D	D	D	D
Breakdown Page #	1-9	10-11	12	13	14-16	17	18	19-22	23-24	25-26	27	28	29	30	31	32	33
Exterior or Interior	E	E	I	E	I	E	E	E	E	I	E	I	E	E	E	E	E
Scene	1-9	10-11	12	13	14-16	17	18	19-22	23-24	25-26	27	28	29	30	31	32	33
Location	UNION SQUARE	UNION SQUARE	PANEL VAN TRUCK	STREET/VAN TRUCK	PANEL VAN TRUCK	EIFFEL TOWER/TOP	EIFFEL TOWER/TOP	UNION SQUARE	OFFICE BLDG. WINDOW	EIFFEL TOWER/TOP	PANEL VAN TRUCK	UNION SQUARE	PANEL VAN TRUCK	EIFFEL TOWER/TOP	OFFICE BLDG WINDOW	UNION SQUARE	UNION SQUARE
No. of Pages	3 3/8	3/8	4/8	1/8	2 1/8	2/8	1 1/8	4/8	5/8	1 2/8	2/8	5/8	1/8	1/8	1/8	1/8	1/8

Character / Artist grid (No. = character number)

Character	Artist	No.	1-9	10-11	12	13	14-16	17	18	19-22	23-24	25-26	27	28	29	30	31	32	33
HARRY CAUL		1	1		1	1							1	2	1				
ANN		2	2	2	2					2	2	2	2	20.V	3				
MARK		3	3		3				30.V	3	3	3	3	30.V					
MR. C.		4																	
STANLEY		5			5		5						5		5				
PAUL MEYERS		6	6							6	6		6						
MARTIN		7																	
WILLIAM P. MORAN		8																	
MEREDITH		9																	
MILLARD		10																	
MRS. GOETNER		11																	
RON. KELLER		12																	
MRS. CORSITTO		13																	
BOB		14																	
BOB'S WIFE		15																	
AMY		16																	
LURLEEN		17																	
MALE SEC'Y (M)	TONY	19																	
MALE RECEPT (20)	MIME (21)		21							21	21	21							21
YOUNG MAN (22)	YOUNG WOMAN (23)		22																
SHOPPER #1 (24)	SHOPPER #2 (25)		23								24								
SHOPPER #3 (26)	LAUNDRY LADY (27)										25								
#27's Little Boy (28)	WOMAN #1-ELEV (29)										26								
WOMAN #2-ELEV (30)	MAN IN ELEVATOR (31)																		
DEMO MAN (32)	SPEAKER (33)		33								(M)								
MAN IN BOOTH (34)	YOUNG DRIVER (35)										(SE)								
MOTEL CLERK (36)	BUS DRIVER #1 (37)				(C)			(SE)			(125)						(C)	(SE)	
BUS DRIVER #2 (38)	McNAUGHT (39)				(SE)						(SE)			(C)			(25)		
ANN'C'R/PA SYST. (40)	TEL.OPER. #1 (41)		(M)		(25)				ROOF#	(50#) / (125)	(50 or 125)	(SE)					(SE)	(25)	
CHROME DOME VO (42)	WOMAN IN R.R.RM (43)		(C)			(C)	(C)			(50 or 125)	(SE)			(125)					
TEL.OPER. #2 (44)	MAN #2 IN BOOTH (45)		(SE)	(SE)			(SE)								(SE)				
			(125)										(125)						

MUSIC : (M)   CARS : (C)
SPECIAL EQUIPMENT : (SE)
ANIMALS : (A)
EXTRAS : (#)

Action / Scene notes (bottom of each column):

1-9	SURVEILLANCE
10-11	CLOSE-UP-ANN
12	SURVEILLANCE OF COUPLE
13	GIRLS FIX MAKE-UP
14-16	DISCUSS SURVEILLANCE
17	SURVEILLANCE FROM ROOF
18	THEY WALK & TALK
19-22	THEY ARE TAILED
23-24	THEY DISCOVER PAUL
25-26	SURVEILLANCE NEAR BONGOS
27	THEY PAY PAUL, LISTEN
28	COUPLE PARTS
29	HARRY MAKES A JOKE
30	LAUGHTER FROM WITHIN
31	MAN PUTS EQUIP. AWAY
32	MAN PACKS EQUIP
33	MUSICIANS PACKUP

Day/Night	Scene	Int/Ext	Location	Pages	Cast / Notes	Action
D	34	E	ELECTRIC BUS	1/8	1?	BUS MOVES ALONG (25)
D	35	I	ELECTRIC BUS	2/8	1	HE EXITS BUS (25) (45)(bus)(25)
D	36–37	E	HARRY'S NEIGHBORHOOD	2/8	1	CROSSES STREET, GOES PARK (20)
D	38	I	NEIGHBORHOOD MARKET	1/8	1 ; 27, 28	SHOPS FOR DINNER (5)
D	39	I	NEIGHBORHOOD LAUNDRY	5/8	1 ; 11	PICKS UP LAUNDRY, MAGIC (A)
D	40	I	HARRY'S APT. BLDG.- FOYER	3/8		CHECKS MAIL, GREETS NEIGHBOR
D	41	I	HARRY'S APARTMENT	1	1 ; 12, 13, 14, 15	HARRY CALLS APT MANAGER
N	42	I	HARRY'S APT. KITCHENETTE	1 7/8	1 ; 12, 13, 14, 15	DISTURBED BY TENANTS
N	43	I	HARRY'S APT. BLDG- FLOOR HALL	3/8	1 ; 11, 12, 13, 14, 15	BOB TALKS TO HARRY
N	44	E	HARRY'S APT.	3 6/8	1	BIRTHDAY PARTY (A)
N	45	I	ELECTRIC BUS	1/8	1	EXITS BUS (10)(C)
N	46	I	AMY'S BLDG - HALL - APT.	2/8	1 ; 16	CLIMBS STAIRS, ENTERS APT
N	47	E	AMY'S APT.	5 3/8	1	HARRY VISITS AMY
N	48	E	HARRY'S APT.	3/8	1	HARRY PLAYS SAX (H)
D	49	I	HARRY'S APT. BLDG.	1/8	1	HARRY EXITS BUILDING
D	50	E	HARRY'S WAREHOUSE	2/8	1	ENTERS H'S WAREHOUSE (25)
D	51–57	I	H'S WAREHOUSE WORK AREA	2 6/8	1, 2, 3, 5	DISCUSS CONVENTION/WORK (H) [REPEAT OPENING - SEE SCENE 9]
D	58	E	UNION SQUARE	5/8	1, 2, 3	C.U. EQUIP./ HARRY (SE)
D	59–61	I	H'S WAREHOUSE WORK AREA	3/8	1, 2, 3, 5 ; 21	[REPEAT OPENING]
D	62	E	UNION SQUARE	3/8	1, 2, 3	LISTENS TO CONVERSATION (SE)
D	63	I	H'S WAREHOUSE WORK AREA	4/8	1, 2, 3, 5	[REPEAT OPENING - SCN #9]
D	64	E	UNION SQUARE	1/8	2	PLAYS IT AGAIN (SE)
D	65	I	H'S WAREHOUSE INDOOR AREA	2/8	1, 2, 3	[REPEAT OR ORIGINAL OPENING] (SE)
D	66	E	UNION SQUARE	3/8	2, 3	HARRY & STANLEY DISAGREE (SE)
D	67	I	H'S WAREHOUSE WORK AREA	3 2/8	1, 2, 3	THEY TALK
D	68	E	UNION SQUARE	7/8	2, 3	WORKS ON FILTERING CONVERSATION
D	69–70	I	H'S WAREHOUSE WORK AREA	4/8	1, 2, 3 ; (SE)	

can double check each element. It takes a little more time, but it is worth catching those few possible mistakes up front.

Caution! Make sure that when you combine scenes (or shots) you do not violate any of the rules (*day/night, interior/exterior, etc*). Sometimes deciding whether two scenes should be put on the same strip is very, very tricky. If in doubt, do not combine scenes.

Keeping all this in mind, go ahead and complete your strips for THE CONVERSATION. When you have finished making all your strips, check your board against the one on the fold out production board. It is a good idea once you have all your strips done to number the strips on the back so that you will know if one is missing.

VI

PARAMETER FACTORS

In deciding what to schedule when, certain factors must be considered. Here, then in order of their priority, is the list.

Parameter Factors
1) Locations
2) Cast Members
3) Day/Night Shooting
4) Exteriors/Interiors
5) Shooting In Sequence
6) Child Actors
7) Changes in Time Periods
8) Time of the Year
9) Weather Conditions
10) Special Effects & Stunts
11) Second Camera and/or Second Unit
12) Special Equipment
13) Geography of Locations
14) Miscellaneous Factors

1) **Locations:** Unless absolutely necessary, you do not want to go back to a location once you have finished with it.

Certain locations will only allow you to film on certain days of the week during certain hours. On a recent film, the production manager had the problem of trying to schedule a scene in the New York Public Library. The Library's policy is to allow filming on the day that it is closed to the public - Thursday. The crew had four weeks in New York to complete shooting. Two of the possible Thursdays were Christmas Eve and New Year's Eve. Because the Library was going to be closed on the two Fridays (Christmas and New Year's), they decided to stay open on those two Thursdays. So, within a four week schedule, there were only two possible days to shoot the scenes in the New York Public Library the Thursday before (Dec. 17th) and the Thursday after (January 6). Suddenly, what started out as an ordinary scene became a major scheduling problem. It took a bit of juggling, but it finally worked out.

2) **Cast Members:** For economic reasons, it is best to try to work an actor's schedule so that you have the fewest number of necessary work days and the fewest number of HOLDING DAYS in between. This also works to the actor's advantage, as he is free to accept other employment as soon as his part is finished.

There are many strict rules concerning actors—we have even separated CHILD ACTORS and given them their own category (#6). Before starting to schedule, it is best to get a copy of the latest edition of the Screen Actors Guild contract and read it. Here are a few key rules which you must know and which will affect your schedule.

>   a)**Always Up-Grade, Never Down-Grade:** During the production of a project, an actor can always be up-graded, never down-graded. For example, an Ex-

tra can move up to a Speaking Part (DAY PLAYER), but a Day Player can never drop to an Extra. A Day Player can be put on a weekly contract, but never vice-versa. And, once that up-grade has been made, it is not reversible on the show.

b) **Drop-And-Pick-Up:** An actor may be "dropped" and "picked-up" only once during a show. Suppose you have a situation where you need a particular actor for three days at the beginning of the schedule and then another five days later on. Unless there are ten free calendar days (with the actor working again on the 11th) you will have to pay the actor for the holding days — the days in-between. The actors are paid at full rate. Suppose that you need this same actor for the time specified above, and an additional four days even later on. If your schedule permits you to drop and pick-up the actor between the first three days and the second five, you will have to pay for all the holding days between the second time he works and the third time.

In some instances, you may find it is less expensive to keep the actor and pay for the holding days because of other PARAMETER FACTORS which if rearranged, could result in higher costs to the film.

c) **Run-Of-Show Deal:** In looking over the list of actors and scene numbers which you used to determine which actor was #1, #2 etc., you may find that an actor is in so many scenes that it makes more sense to have him around for the entire show. This kind of deal is called a RUN-OF-SHOW DEAL and pays the actor a certain amount for a certain number of weeks' work—no matter how many or how few days he works within those weeks. Harry Caul is an example of an actor who should have a run-of-show deal. If the project involves a well-known actor, then the producers have probably already made this deal. This will eliminate this actor as a major scheduling problem. You may find that it is the smaller parts which prove to be the most difficult scheduling problems.

Run-of-show deals never become drop-and-pick-up.

d) **Special Clauses:** Some actors have special clauses in their contracts which determine the amount of time they may work during the day; or that they cannot start before such-and-such a time or must end work by such-and-such a time. If the actor is hired under these conditions, then the rules must be adhered to.

3) **Day And Night Shooting:** When you lay out your locations, keep in mind that you cannot schedule a full "day's" work after finishing a full "night's" work. Most of the Unions and Guilds have very strict rules concerning TURN-AROUND TIME—the minimum number of time-off a person must have before coming back to work. For example, during the week—an actor must have twelve hours off from the time he leaves the set and returns to work. Travel to and from the location must be added in if the location is not considered a local location. He must have 58 uninterrupted hours from the completion of Friday's work to Monday's work. If Friday was a night shoot, then the actors and crew will need a minimum amount of uninterrupted free time before they may report back to

work. Any violation of these hours results in having to pay a **PENALTY**—very expensive and should be avoided unless absolutely necessary. Each Union/Guild has its own rules, and as you guessed, not too many of them are similar.

As for shooting at night, it is best to try to schedule your night work on a Friday (if working a five-day week) or even block out an entire week for night work. Switching from day shooting to night shooting causes the same kind of jet lag and slowness which you experience when flying across the country. Don't expect to accomplish the same amount of work at night.

4) **Exteriors/Interiors:** It is a good idea to always shoot your exteriors before moving inside. Although Production Managers try to control as many of the variables as possible, there is one variable that cannot be controlled—sun, or lack of it. It is much easier, except in certain unusual circumstances, to **DRESS** windows so as to give the appearance of night when filming a night interior in the day time than it is to create the illusion of night when filming outside.

5) **Shooting in Sequence:** Whenever possible, try to shoot all of the scenes in one location in sequential order. If an actor is required to build to an emotional point at the end of the scene, it will be easier for the actor and for the director if the sequence is shot in order.

Sometimes, however, it is just not possible to shoot in sequence. Take a location which has many windows facing west on one side of the room. If you were trying to film in that location in winter, you would find that the light in the room would change almost continuously and that you

59

would lose your light very quickly. Because of the nature of the location, you are going to be forced to shoot all the scenes facing the window at one time of day and all the other ones either before or after. This problem could add extra days to the location and possibly to the schedule.

6) **Child Actors:** As we mentioned under Cast Members, rules for child actors are quite strict. Depending on the age of the child (or children), a TEACHER or WELFARE WORKER may be necessary. The hours a child actor may work and under what conditions are very strict. Make sure that you consult with the Screen Actors Guild before trying to schedule a child actor.

7) **Changes In Time Period:** If a script is set in any other time period but the present day, a certain amount of time must be spent to ensure that all the elements fit the period of time you are depicting. It looks out of place to have a 1930's movie with 1980's streetlights. Or, a futuristic film with everyday street clothes. Special make-up and wardrobe may be needed; sets have to be specially constructed, etc. All this requires time—time which must be allotted and scheduled.

In THE REINCARNATION OF PETER PROUD, the house (location) had to be shown in two different time periods—thirty years apart. In the present day scenes, the house had to be shown in a state of disrepair, almost decay. The paint was faded and chipped, and dust-covered cloths were on the furniture. It had to look as if no one had lived there for many years. In the flashback scenes (1940's), the house had to look brand new. The actress, Margot Kidder, played an elderly woman in present day and herself as a young woman in the flashbacks. Preparing both Ms. Kidder and the house were scheduling problems with which we had to contend. The house was shot first, present day, in its delapidated state. Then the shooting crew moved out and the art department moved in. About two weeks later, the shooting crew returned to a new-looking house, freshly painted inside and out. We shot the 1940's sequence. It required about two additional hours to make Ms. Kidder up to portray the elderly woman. On those days, we shot other scenes first so as not to always give Ms. Kidder an exceptionally early make-up call.

8) **Time Of Year Filming:** As mentioned in an earlier example, winter months in the Northern Hemisphere mean less light. (Just the opposite in the Southern Hemisphere). As you move further north in winter, you will have less and less daylight. Take into consideration any unusual weather problems which you may encounter during the particular time of year—snow, rain, tornadoes, hurricanes, etc. In one part of California, the fog is so bad during some winter months that it is almost impossible to see. Knowing this will allow you to plan for the almost sure delays you will encounter. Call your local library, or better yet go there and check out the weather maps. Also, check *The Farmer's Almanac* (published annually every October).

9) **Weather:** This factor can and does add more time to a winter picture where cold weather can affect not only movement of people and equipment, but also the film through the camera. Productions move more slowly in extreme cold weather—especially at night.

10) **Special Effects & Stunts:** Depending on what is required for your project, it may require a lot of additional prepara-

tion time for Stunts and/or Special Effects. Especially on science-fiction films, many of the special effects will have to be created by computers. At this writing, there is one project which is about to begin eleven months of preparation and graphics work before they begin pre-production on the principal photography. The eleven months preparation is only for the computer generated images!

11) **Second Camera And/Or Second Unit:** SECOND CAMERA is an additional camera which shoots at the same time and on the same scene as the first camera. SECOND UNIT is an additional camera which shoots scenes other than what is being shot by the FIRST UNIT and does not include principal actors. A good way of compressing your time schedule is to use a second camera. However, it is not always the panacea that it appears to be. Some directors are not comfortable with a second camera. You will also need extra lighting as you will be lighting for two, not just one. Sometimes, if the second camera operation is not properly scrutinized, it can actually cost you time and money.

In THE CONVERSATION, Coppola and the production department agreed to use a second camera for the first two weeks. As you can tell from reading the script, many of the scenes which appear later in the story are actually different angles of scenes which appear earlier in the story. Having two cameras run simultaneously saved enormous amounts of time which would have been wasted had they needed to wait for the crew to move the camera to another SET-UP.

A Second Unit can be helpful. A true Second Unit has its own SECOND UNIT DIRECTOR, SECOND UNIT DIRECTOR OF PHOTOGRAPHY, and other key department heads. The production can break away some of their key members from First Unit and raise them to higher positions on Second Unit. For example, a SECOND ASSISTANT DIRECTOR on First Unit could be the First A.D. on Second Unit. Much depends on how independent the Second Unit is from the First Unit. In the case of *THE CONVERSATION* it was decided to keep the second camera as close to the First Unit as possible, and not let them actually break off and become a Second Unit.

In scripts which contain a lot of action and/or large crowd scenes, it is good to schedule additional cameras. But why be concerned here with additional cameras? You are going to need to know that the schedule you lay out is workable, that the amount of work (# of pages) you say can be shot in a day can actually be shot in a day. A second camera can aid in completing the day's (or night's) work. Each individual script together with the preferences of the director within the parameters of the budget will determine whether or not additional cameras are used.

12) **Special Equipment:** Wolfgang Glattes (co-producer STAR '80) was at one time involved with the film THE BOAT (*DAS BOOT*). When he was preparing his schedule, the availability of the German submarine was as important as the availability of any other parameter factor. In effect, the boat itself was considered to be a Cast Member.

You may find that you are going to need a SPECIAL PORTABLE CAMERA (e.g., Steadicam or Panaglide), and therefore, a SPECIAL CAMERA OPERATOR. Both the camera and the operator have to be scheduled as they are not always available and are quite costly. (Sometimes you will find that your camera operator is capable of operating the special camera, so you will only have to worry about the availability of the camera, not the operator.) A similar example can be made with HELICOPTER SHOTS. Not only do you need to rent a helicopter with a special camera mount, but also to hire a HELICOPTER PILOT who has flown helicopters to shoot films before and a HELICOPTER CAMERA OPERATOR.

13) **Geography of Location:** Sometimes the geography of the location can dictate the schedule lay-out. If the locations are spread all over the place, then hopefully the key locations will take precedence and it will be necessary to find alternate SECONDARY LOCATIONS closer to the PRIMARY LOCATIONS. For example, Harry's Warehouse (if actually shot on location) is a primary location whereas Amy's Apartment is a secondary location. If a suitable location is found for Harry's Warehouse but it is very far from Amy's Apartment location, unless there is a very good reason for not finding an alternate, a back-up location will be found for Amy's Apartment.

14) **Miscellaneous Factors:** You will come across other elements and factors which will affect the planning of your project. Always allow for the unexpected—your individual project will determine that.

VII

ARRANGING THE BOARD

Now that you understand the Parameter Factors, the first step in organizing your board will be to line up all your strips by location. Put all of the Union Square strips together in one space, all of Harry's Warehouse together, etc. Within each location, separate out the DAY and NIGHT material and put them together. Keep the strips in chronological order wherever possible. Use some of the black strips as dividers.

Don't by-pass this step and go on to the next step. This is a very important part of creating your production board.

Take the time now and arrange your board by locations. Please refer to the example in this chapter if you are unsure.

Once you have arranged the strips by location, you can now begin arranging them by cast within the various locations. By running your finger horizontally along the strips, you will see where each actor PLAYS (appears). Look for patterns. The first that you will see is that Stanley and Paul usually appear together, as do Mark and Ann. The only time all four actors appear together is in the UNION SQUARE sequence. Remembering that once you start an actor there must be enough drop-and-pick-up days in-between, you can see what would happen if you started your show with Union Square—either Ann and Mark or Stanley and Paul are going to do a lot of waiting around to complete their parts. As a result, you might be forced to return to a location later in the schedule to complete the actor's work. Such a DOUBLE-MOVE should be avoided. Also, it is better not to start the schedule with such a complicated scene. Give everyone time to get to know each other and work the bugs out before starting this.

As you can see, there are several scenes in which Harry works either alone or with characters who are in only one or two relatively small scenes, e.g., McNaught (the attorney), Harry's neighbors at *Harry's Apartment,* Amy at *Amy's Apartment,* etc. These scenes can be moved around the schedule with more flexibility than extremely complicated scenes or scenes involving other major characters.

Judging from the material in the script and the complexity of the plot, this is going to be an interesting screenplay to schedule. Go through your board and start grouping together the scenes which involve Harry alone, Harry with a minor character, Harry with Ann and/or Mark, Harry with Stanley and/or Paul. Just to keep things fairly straight here, group all Harry-alone scenes in the front of the board, and all Harry with minor-character scenes at the end of the board. In the middle put Harry with Ann/Mark, Harry with Ann/Mark/Stanley/Paul etc., and then Harry with Stanley/Paul. Put all miscellaneous scenes, especially the ones in which Harry doesn't appear at the end of the board, or in with the other scenes at the same location. Use your black strips to separate the locations. You may find that you are working with both ends of the board at the same time, going towards the middle.

Keep arranging and refining your board according to the Parameter Factors until you think that you have arrived at the best possible order. Don't start separating your board into days yet. One big question will loom up rather quickly—when to shoot the Union Square sequence? As you know from reading the screenplay several times, this is a key sequence. Should we do it right off and get it out of the way? We made the decision to schedule the Union Square sequence before the Warehouse sequence. Why? If you re-read the Warehouse sequence, you will see that Harry is going to play tapes of THE CONVERSA- TION in the warehouse. In order for him to actually play those tapes, they are going to have to be **PRE-RECORDED**. It is possi- ble that they could be pre-recorded in pre-production, or even dubbed in afterwards. However, in order to approach reality more closely, Mr. Coppola decided to record all the necessary dialogue on location so that not only would the actor's dialogue be recorded, so would all the requisite background noise. Therefore, we know that Ann and Mark's scenes in Union Square are going to have to be shot first so that there will be time enough to have the tapes and the still photographs of Ann and Mark by the time the warehouse is scheduled. Taking into consideration that the weather will be growing considerably worse as December approaches and that the Director needs a Christmas look, the Union Square sequence will have to be scheduled fairly early.

Now, keeping this in mind, see if you can roughly lay out your board. If you get stuck, refer to the Production Board fold-out.

Title: THE CONVERSATION
Director: FRANCIS COPPOLA
Producer:
Asst. Director:
PROD'N MGR: CLARK PAYLOW

Scene column	1	2	3	4	5	6	7	8	9	10	11	12	13	14	15	16
Day or Nite	N	N	D	D	D	D	D	D	N	N	N	N	D	N	D	N
Breakdown Page #	46	47	104	105	106	108	40	41	42	43	44	48	49	377	380-397	378-379
Exterior or Interior	I	I	E	I	I	I	I	I	I	I	I	I	E	I	I	I
Scene #	46	47	104	105	106	108	40	41	42	43	44	48	49	377	380-397	378-379
Location	AMY'S BLDG-HALL-APT.	AMY'S APT.	AMY'S APT. BLDG	AMY'S BLDG-HALL	AMY'S APT.	AMY'S APT	HARRY'S APT. BLDG-FOYER	HARRY'S APARTMENT	HARRY'S APT.-KITCHENETTE	HARRY'S APT. BLDG-Floor Hall	HARRY'S APT.	HARRY'S APT.	HARRY'S APT BLDG.	HARRY'S APT. BLDG	HARRY'S APARTMENT	HARRY'S APARTMENT
No. of Pages	2/8	5 3/8	1/8	2/8	1 3/8	1/8	3/8	1	1 7/8	3/8	3 5/8	3/8	1/8	4/8	2 7/8	3

Character	No.	1	2	3	4	5	6	7	8	9	10	11	12	13	14	15	16
HARRY CAUL	1	/	/		/	/	/	/	/	/	/	/	/	/	/	/	/
ANN	2				2 V.O.	2 V.O.											
MARK	3					3 V.O.											3 V.O.
MR. C.	4																
STANLEY	5																
PAUL MEYERS	6																
MARTIN	7																
WILLIAM P. MORAN	8																
MEREDITH	9																
MILLARD	10																
MRS. GOETNER	11							11				11					
RON KELLER	12									12	12	12					12
MRS. CORSITTO	13										13	13					
BOB	14									14	14	14					14
BOB'S WIFE	15									15	15	15					
AMY	16	16 V.O., 16															
LURLEEN	17																

Additional cast (paired):

Character	No.	Character	No.
MALE SEC'Y	18	TONY	19
MALE RECEPT.	20	MIME	21
YOUNG MAN	22	YOUNG WOMAN	23
SHOPPER #1	24	SHOPPER #2	25
SHOPPER #3	26	LAUNDRY LADY	27
#27'S LITTLEBOY	28	WOMAN #1-ELEV	29
WOMAN #2-ELEV	30	MAN IN ELEVATOR	31
DEMO MAN	32	SPEAKER	33
MAN IN BOOTH	34	YOUNG DRIVER	35
MOTEL CLERK	36	BUS DRIVER #1	37
BUS DRIVER #2	38	MC NAUGHT	39
ANNC'R/PA SYS.	40	TEL. OPER. #1	41
CHROME DOME V.O.	42	WOMAN IN R'RM	43
TEL. OPER. #2	44	MAN #2 IN BOOTH	45

(MALE SEC'Y 18: column 16 = 18 V.O.)

Legend:
MUSIC: Ⓜ
SPECIAL EQUIPMENT: (SE)
ANIMALS: Ⓐ
EXTRAS: (#)
CARS: Ⓒ

Column markings: col 3 ⑩ ; col 7 Ⓐ ; col 10 Ⓐ ; col 13 Ⓜ ; col 15 "* THE END *"

Action notes (by column):
1 CLIMBS STAIRS, ENTERS APT — 2 HARRY VISITS AMY — 3 ENTERS BLDG — 4 OPENS AMY'S DOOR — 5 AMY'S GONE — 6 STAND IN EMPTY APT. — 7 CHECKS MAIL, GREETS NEIGHBOR — 8 HARRY CALLS APT. MANAGER — 9 DISTURBED BY TENANTS — 10 BOB TALKS TO HARRY — 11 BIRTHDAY PARTY — 12 HARRY PLAYS SAX — 13 HARRY EXITS BUILDING — 14 PASSES RON ON STAIRCASE — 15 SEARCHES FOR WIRETAP — 16 TRIES MR. C'S OFFICE, CONFRONTS NEIGHBORS

D	D		D	D	D	D	D	D	D	D	D	D	N	N	N	N	N	N	N	N	N	N	N	N	D
93-94	95		50	51-57	59-61	63	65	67	69-70	72-80	82-86	88-91	160	161-173	174-181	183-184	186-187	333-336	337-339	340-353	355	357-358	362	364	230
I	I		E	I	I	I	I	I	I	I	I	I	I	I	I	I	E	I	I	I	I	I	I	I
93-94	95		50	51-57	59-61	63	65	67	69-70	72-80	82-86	91	160	161-173	174-181	183-184	186-187	333-336	337-339	340-353	355	357-358	362	364	230
LAWYER'S OFFICE	LAWYER'S OFF. & STUDY		HARRY'S WARE HOUSE	H'S WAREHOUSE WORK AREA	H'S WARE HOUSE WORK AREA	H'S WARE HOUSE WORK AREA	H'S WAREHOUSE WORK AREA	H'S WARE HOUSE WORK AREA	H'S WARE HOUSE WORK AREA	H'S WARE HOUSE WORK AREA	H'S WARE HOUSE WORK AREA	H'S WARE HOUSE WORK AREA	H'S WARE HOUSE WORK AREA	H'S WARE HOUSE WORK AREA	H'S WARE HOUSE WORK AREA	H'S WARE HOUSE WORK AREA	H'S WARE HOUSE WORK AREA	H'S WARE HOUSE – ALLEY	H'S WARE HOUSE – STAIRCASE	HARRY'S WARE HOUSE	H'S WARE HOUSE – WORK AREA	H'S WARE HOUSE – WORK AREA	H'S WARE HOUSE – WORK AREA	H'S WARE HOUSE – WORK AREA	CATHOLIC CHURCH
2 3/8	2 7/8		2/8	2 4/8	3/8	4/8	3/8	3 3/8	2 5/8	1 3/8	3/8	1	1/8	1/8	19 7/8	9 7/8	2/8	5/8	4/8	3/8	3 3/8	2/8	3/8	1/8	1/8	2/8

1	1		1		1	1	1	1	1	1		1		1	1	1	1	1	1	1	1	1	1	1	1
				2v.o.		2v.o.	2v.o.	2v.o.	2v.o.2 v.o.	2v.o.				2v.o.	2v.o.						2v.o.		2v.o.	2v.o.	
				3v.o.	3v.o.	3v.o.	3v.o.	3v.o.	3.o.3.o.	3v.o.					3v.o.						3v.o.	3v.o.	3v.o.		
				5		5		5						5											
										6v.o.	6.														
										9v.o.	9.	9													
											10.														
											17														
	19																								

Scene descriptions (bottom):

Column	Scene marker	Description
LAWYER'S OFFICE	39	REVEALED AS OWNER/SEES TONY
LAWYER'S OFF. & STUDY		TONY CRIES, TELLS STORY
HARRY'S WARE HOUSE	(25)	ENTERS HIS WARE HOUSE
H'S WAREHOUSE WORK AREA	(SE)	DISCUSS CONVENTION/WORK
H'S WARE HOUSE WORK AREA	(SE)	C.U. EQUIP./HARRY
H'S WARE HOUSE WORK AREA		LISTENS TO CONVERSATION
H'S WAREHOUSE WORK AREA	(SE)	PLAYS IT AGAIN
H'S WARE HOUSE WORK AREA	(SE)	HARRY + STANLEY DISAGREE
H'S WARE HOUSE WORK AREA	(SE)	WORKS ON FILTERING CONVERSATION
H'S WARE HOUSE WORK AREA	(SE)	WORKS ON CONVERSATION
H'S WARE HOUSE WORK AREA	(SE)	WORKS ON CONVERSATION
H'S WARE HOUSE WORK AREA	(SE)	WORKS ON CONVERSATION
H'S WARE HOUSE WORK AREA	(SE)(M)	EST. SHOT- WORK AREA
H'S WARE HOUSE WORK AREA	(SE)	THEY PARTY, LEAVE
H'S WARE HOUSE WORK AREA	(SE)	THEY LISTEN, SLEEP
H'S WARE HOUSE WORK AREA		REEL TURNS, HARRY SLEEPS
H'S WARE HOUSE WORK AREA	(SE)	AWAKENS-MEREDITH'S GONE
H'S WARE HOUSE WORK AREA		DISCOVERS BREAK IN
H'S WARE HOUSE – ALLEY		CLIMBS STAIRS
H'S WARE HOUSE – STAIRCASE	(SE)	CHASES INTRUDER AWAY
HARRY'S WARE HOUSE		HARRY LISTENS, REMEMBERS
H'S WARE HOUSE – WORK AREA		STARES AT PLAYING TAPE
H'S WARE HOUSE – WORK AREA	(SE)	LISTENS TO TAPE
H'S WARE HOUSE – WORK AREA	(SE)	TURNS OFF RECORDER
CATHOLIC CHURCH	(10)	GOES TO CONFESSION

VIII
HOW MANY DAYS?

Now that you have arranged your board according to the Parameter Factors, you can start to determine the amount of time it is going to take to film each location.

Until now, most of the work was manual—lining the script, filling in the breakdown sheets and preparing the strips. Now comes the hard part—determining how much time everything is going to need. Unfortunately, there is no real formula and your ability to guess correctly will improve with experience.

If the director has not been hired, ask the producers whom they have in mind and then do some research. Find out what the director (or director-candidate) has done in the past and speak to those in production (production manager). To find out what a director's most recent credits are, either look in *FILM DIRECTORS: A Complete Guide (Lone Eagle Publishing)* or call the Directors Guild of America (if the director is a member of the DGA). You will probably need to call the production companies to find out who the production manager and/or assistant directors were on the show. Ask the production manager and/or the A.D. how the director organizes his work. *Does he stay on schedule? Has the director done this kind of material before? Does the director work well with actors? What about action scenes?* If you are blessed, you will be fortunate to be working with a director who does both well—actors and action. Ask more questions—*How long a day does the director like to work?* Some directors, like Sidney Lumet, are well organized and like to go home at a reasonable time. These are but a few questions you should ask those who have experienced the director before. Always remember that you must weigh the director's past work. A key rule: The director always sets the pace on the set.

Next, you should ask the producer and director (if hired) whom they have in mind as **DIRECTOR OF PHOTOGRAPHY**. The **DP** (called **DOP** in England and Australia) is a key person and his methods of shooting can and do play a major role in determining how much time it is going to take to shoot each scene. There are DP's who take a great deal of time to light a set (the term "location" is interchangeable here), and then there are others, especially those who have a strong television background who move quickly through the scripted material. If you can find out who is being considered, then you will be able to create a more workable, realistic schedule.

We are scheduling a five-day work week (Monday through Friday) because THE CONVERSATION is considered an **IN-TOWN** show, and not a **LOCATION PICTURE** which uses a six-day (Monday through Saturday) schedule. This will make more of a difference in budgeting then in scheduling.

Start with scenes involving only Harry (if possible). Try to give the actor and the director some working time together. Stay away from scenes which involve heavy preparation (action, special effects, make-up, stunts, large numbers of principal actors, crowd scenes, intimate or highly emotional scenes, etc.) Since principal photography has been scheduled for late November, just after Thanksgiving, it would be wise to do as many exteriors as possible. In January, the weather (even in San Francisco) isn't the best. Although you can plan your schedule for any time period during the year, we thought it would be more interesting to schedule this show over the same time period that it was actually shot.

In looking over the board and taking all the Parameters into consideration, here, then is the schedule which we feel works best.

DAY 1 -
Sunday, November 26

EXT. - Financial District - DAY (195 - 198) 5/8
EXT. - Financial District Phone Booth - DAY (226 - 229) 4/8
EXT. - Golden Gate Park - DAY (188 - 194) 2-3/8
Total - 3-4/8 pages

The first day of the schedule and we have already broken a rule: we're starting on Sunday, not Monday. You have a location—the Financial District—which has to look two ways: active and desolate. Short of stopping all traffic and business in that area to shoot the necessary scenes during the week, the only way to accomplish this is to shoot it on a weekend when offices are closed and the streets will be empty. Since you are going to have your crew available and working on Sunday, and you are going to have to pay them the minimum call, it makes sense to schedule more than just one little 1/8 of a page scene. Refer to your script, when Harry walks into the Financial District building and into the empty elevator area (Scene 198). This scene would also be difficult to stage on a normally busy day. After Harry's meeting upstairs with Mr. C., we see him walking through a bleak and desolate financial district (Scenes 226 - 229). He stops and makes a phone call. In the script, you will find an earlier scene in which Harry confronts Stanley. He does this in Scenes 188 - 194 in Golden Gate Park—on a Sunday. This is more of a coincidence than a deciding factor, but it gives you another scene which can be shot that same day. Ok, now, *which* Sunday. If you begin on a Sunday, then you will avoid the TURN-AROUND problem which would face you if you tried to shoot this after having worked on the previous Friday. So, let's schedule it first and get it over with. Remember that you are going to have to give your actors a certain number of hours off before they can work again. If you do not do this, you will find yourself in a FORCED CALL situation—not giving them enough time off—and having to pay dearly for it.

If you tried to shoot this Sunday sequence later on in the schedule, you would be severely limiting the material you could shoot in the latter part of the week before. Keeping possible weather problems in mind, it makes sense to get this over with first.

As we stated—shooting on a Sunday is an exception, not a rule. If you are looking for an average, or more normal way to start a shooting schedule, then begin on a Wednesday. It gives the director and crew a couple of days to get used to each other, renew old acquaintances etc., and then two days off before you get into full swing. It also gives the cast and crew the time during the early part of the week to make any last minute necessary changes before DAY ONE.

The page count for the day is an ambitious 3-4/8 pages.

DAY 2
Monday, November 27.

EXT. Electric Bus/Neighborhood - DAY (34, 36, 37) - 3/8
INT. Electric Bus - DAY (35) - 2/8

INT. Market - DAY (38) - 1/8
Total - 6/8 pages.

It is Monday. We are going to do more exterior work with
Harry alone. In order to film the inside of the market, it will
probably be necessary for the crew to go in and PRE-LIGHT
(take out the flourescent light bulbs and replace them with
color-corrected bulbs, hang additional lights, etc.) and PRE-RIG
(put up any scaffolding, ceiling mounts for the lights). Part of
the crew can be working on this while the other part of the crew
is working on the Exteriors and the Interior of the Bus. Although 6/8 of a page doesn't seem like very much, laying out
street action and coordinating it is not an easy task, especially
considering the light availability problem at this time of the
year. This will be a busy second day's work.

DAY 3
Tuesday, November 28

EXT. Street - Burning Car - DAY (365) 1/8
EXT. Electric Bus - NIGHT (45) 1/8
Total - 2/8 pages.

Mr. C. (*Robert Duvall*) works in three distinctly different locations—his office, the motel room and the burning Mercedes
Benz. Your question to the director should be, "Does the person in the burning car have to be the actor or can it be a STUNT
PHOTO DOUBLE?" (a stunt person who closely resembles the
actor). If a photo double can be used, then you have more
flexibility in scheduling the time to shoot this scene. In this case,
both the producer and the director wanted Duvall to be in the
scene and not doubled. Until now, we have not STARTED any
other key actor except for Stanley. Based upon the special
effects requirements and control which will be mandatory by

the Police and Fire Departments, and since this is a Day Exterior, it would be advisable to do this scene as early as possible in the schedule. Mr. C may be your first drop-and-pick-up. Keep that in mind as you schedule his next work—making sure that you keep at least ten calendar days between his last day of work and the next day of work. Most likely, Ann and Mark will have started working and you will be able to schedule one of Mr. C.'s two remaining scenes then.

The burning car scene will have to be shot in a remote area approved by the local authorities. This forces the film crew to pack up and move after completing the scene. Because of the loss of time and resulting loss of light, it makes sense to schedule a Night Exterior. Keep in mind that it must be a simple one in order to finish early. If we film late into the night, we will face a possible turn-around problem the next day. Since we were filming the Electric Bus sequence the day before and the cast, crew, director, etc., are all familiar with it, why not schedule it for this day and get Scene 45 - Exterior Electric Bus - Night, out of the way? It only involves Harry and has a value of 1/8 of a page.

DAY 4
Wednesday, November 29

EXT. Financial District - DAY (96, 97) 2/8
EXT. Financial Plaza - DAY (271, 272) 2/8
EXT. Director's Bldg. - DAY (282, 283) 3/8
Total - 7/8 pages

With the aim of finishing our Day Exteriors as early into the schedule as possible, we return to a location: Financial District, Plaza - Director's Building. Here we are barely four days into a schedule and we have already broken two rules which we gave you. The first, we started our schedule on a Sunday and now we are returning to a location. If you look at the scenes for this location you will see that we need two completely different looks—one busy and one desolate. As we mentioned before, it would take a lot of work and probably cost more money to try to shoot both of these looks at the same time. Therefore, it makes more sense to return.

In Scenes 96 and 97, Harry walks across the busy street, through the plaza towards the escalator. In Scene 271, Harry moves quickly through the crowded Financial Plaza. In 272, we see Harry's POV of the Director's building in the Plaza. In Scene 282, Ann walks out of the Director's building and down the street. Harry follows her. In Scene 283, Ann walks toward and boards an Electric Bus. Harry follows and boards the bus behind. Scenes 96, 97, 271, 272, 282 and 283 all require a crowded plaza. Therefore, we have scheduled these scenes together. In Scene 283, the script calls for "low fog". This would be noted on your breakdown sheets and would be a question you would ask your director.

DAYS 5,6
Thursday, November 30; Friday, December 1

EXT. Union Square - DAY.
(1-9, 58, 62, 64, 66, 68, 71, 87, 107) - 6-7/8.
Total - 6-7/8 pages

The key sequence for this film is UNION SQUARE where "the conversation" takes place. It is all exterior day work. Scenes and voice-overs of Ann and Mark's conversation at this location are used throughout the remainder of the screenplay. At first glance, you may think that Scenes 62, 64 etc., are merely repeats of Scene 9. On further inspection and analysis, however, we see the subtle difference which make this script so fascinating, and so complicated to do. Be careful. Don't automatically call a scene a repeat unless it is *exactly* the same.

As mentioned earlier, when at all possible, it is best to shoot all scenes at a certain location in sequential order. It works to the director's and actors' advantage—allowing them to build a performance. It is also quite helpful in MATCHING.

We shall continue using a second camera to get the necessary COVERAGE for the work we have scheduled. Alfred Hitchcock once said that a motion picture is merely a series of still photographs. This sequence in Union Square is an excellent illustration. Through proper and thorough coverage, a series of scenes works throughout the entire film. It should be noted that coverage of a scene should be laid out intelligently. Excessive shooting of angles which are not used in the completed editing are a waste of time and money.

In THE CONVERSATION, Mr. Coppola has given the reader just enough information to form an opinion. As the story progresses, we learn more and more through Harry and find out that what we thought we heard—that the "poor young couple. Ann and Mark," who are deeply in love and are in danger of being found out—is not really true at all. Actually the "poor young couple" is using Harry Caul in their plot to murder Ann's husband, Mr. C. Through Harry, they force Mr. C. into a neutral, unguarded location where they can , and do, murder him. As the story progresses, we finally figure this all out and realize that Harry has been used. How did Mr. Coppola do this? The board tells us all the scripted scene numbers for the Union Square sequence. Let's go deeper and analyze the surveillance of "the conversation" and see how that "conversation" was written. We shall begin with Scene 1.

Scene 1
We begin with a MEDIUM SHOT (View) of EXT. Union Square. A small band of street musicians have just set up in the park.

Scene 2
HIGH FULL SHOT (wide) establishing the downtown area of San Francisco. The Union Square is in the center of the frame. From the script we know that it is lunchtime on a workday sometime close to Christmas. Both are established in this shot through wardrobe, set dressing and props.

Scene 3
Here Coppola planned to begin his MAIN TITLES. The camera begins to ZOOM in on the park at Union Square. The shot ends on the Young Mime who is imitating certain passers-by walking down a walkway.

Scene 4
The camera goes to a close shot (view) of the musicians we saw in Scene 1. One musician puts down his instrument and begins to tap dance.

Scene 5
The camera draws in to a close shot (view) of the tapping shoes.

Scene 6
A shot of the mime imitating a middle-aged man who is OFF-CAMERA.

Scene 7
The director shows us who the mime is imitating, and introduces HARRY CAUL—the main character of the film.

Scene 8
The camera cuts back to the musicians. The saxophonist is playing a solo. The crowd, including Harry, is delighted. The musicians play, "Red, Red Robin."

Scene 9

Two other lead characters are introduced—ANN and MARK. We see them pass Harry and join the spectators watching the band. They make a few comments. Ann sings along a few lines of "Red, Red Robin." They walk away, leaving Harry. They come upon an old derelict asleep on a park bench. Ann is upset. They talk about the derelict and then move on. They pass Harry again, talking. This time, however, the sound is coming from off-screen. As Ann and Mark pass, Harry gets up off the bench where he is sitting and walks toward a small panel van truck. The camera moves up the face of the building to the roof where we see a man holding a shotgun microphone. We hear what he is listening to—Ann and Mark's conversation.

From this point, we would not go on to Scene 10 because it would require a major camera move to the roof of the building to see the scene from his point of view. What about having a second camera on the roof? Well, the only problem would be that if you shot Scene 9 in one continuous take and there were a camera on the roof, you would run into the possibility of seeing the camera in the end of the shot.

As you will see when you look at the Shooting Schedule in Chapter IX, the work for Days 5 & 6 has been divided into two sections—Scenes 1-9 and the rest of the scenes. Notice also that Harry is not listed on the schedule for the scenes after 1-9. In reading the script closely, you will see that Harry is not really needed. The mention of him in Scene 58 is actually a repeat of scene 9. Since Harry Caul is a run-of-show player, the director felt that it would be best to give him a few days off. He is not needed again until Day 10.

Scene 58

This scene is intercut into the Warehouse sequence where Harry studies the tapes. This scene will appear in the film, but notice that Ann and Mark's dialogue appears to be coming off-screen. This tells us that the dialogue we are hearing for this part of Scene 9 was recorded from somewhere else so as to give a feeling of surveillance.

Scene 62
Again, we find Ann and Mark repeating lines which we heard in Scene 9, but this time there is a difference. Here as Harry works on making a better recording, he brings out dialogue which we haven't heard before. This is new information which actually expands what we heard and saw in Scene 9.

Scene 64
In Scene 9, Ann and Mark walk up to an old derelict. This is a piece of coverage of that scene which is not used until now in the chronology of the film.

Scene 66
In Scene 9, Ann and Mark walk past the derelict. Additional dialogue is introduced. This is a new scene and again, part of the coverage of Scene 9 but used later in the script and noted with a new scene number. Again, Harry is building "the conversation" through the use of electronics.

Scene 68
Here, we have two lines, *MARK: "Where'd you hear that?"* in *Scene 18* and, *MARK: "It's a nice day today; yesterday it was cold and foggy,"* - Scene 22. Scene 18 as you see is a scene to be shot from the roof of the building. Scene 22 is of Paul following Ann and Mark. Scene 68 does not include Paul. We see the Mime in the background imitating Ann and Mark. As you see in Scene 19, which we are also not doing now, the Mime does his imitation to the crowd's amusement. Scene 68 actually gives us coverage of the surveillance from Scene 17 where we get some dialogue to the middle of Scene 22. This additional

coverage leads us through Harry's eventual discovery of Ann and Mark's plot.

Scene 71
This is a close shot of Ann which widens to include Mark. Paul passes by in the shot. This is actually coverage of the end of Scene 22, "An expression of fear comes to her (Ann's) face", and Scene 24 (telescopic view from the roof of the building.) Ann remarks to Mark about the man with the hearing aid and Mark tries to comfort her.

Scene 87
This is additional dialogue for Scene 27. *MARK: "You go..."* *ANN: "You really don't, but I want to kiss you."* This scene is on Ann and Mark and part of the dialogue is used as off-screen lines inside the Panel Van Truck.

Scene 107
This scene is actually the last part of Scene 87. This could be a separate SET-UP from Scene 87 of Ann leaning forward and giving Mark a kiss as she is about to deliver her line.

All these scenes keep us at ground level on the Square. It is obvious that it will take more than one day, but it should not take more than two. How does one arrive at that conclusion. Well, let's look at the factors. We have six pages of material to do. There are four principal actors involved and, with the exception of contracting the Square for SET-UPS (Camera moves), the dialogue should not take more than two days.

You have now completed Week One. You will continue working on the Union Square material on Monday, since you have probably run out of light now after having completed six pages.

DAY 7
Monday, December 4

EXT. Union Square - DAY (Scene 19-22, 81, 28, 33, 182, 185, 222) 2-4/8
Total - 2-4/8 pages.

It's Monday morning and we are back in Union Square. As we said before, you should continue with a location lowest scene number first.

Scene 19
We're staying at ground level so the first scene is 19. The Mime does a burlesque of Ann and Mark

Scenes 20, 21 and 22
The sequence continues in Scene 20, a MOVING VIEW of Ann and Mark who do not see the Mime's imitation of them. We introduce Paul in Scene 21. This leads us to Scene 22 where we see Paul trying to stay close to Ann and Mark in order to pick up their conversation. This part of the ground level sequence ends when Ann notices Paul. He realizes that he has been pointed out and passes by, hoping to avoid further interest. The sequence shifts to a shot from high up in an open window which will be done, once we complete all the ground level material. We did not try to schedule this material on Friday because we probably would have run out of light and the scenes wouldn't have matched.

Scene 81
Time to break another rule again "Try to shoot in sequence at a location." Chronologically, Scene 81 should be shot later on. However, as we can read from the script, Scene 81 is actually

coverage of Scene 26 (telescopic view from the roof of the building) but with additional dialogue. Ann and Mark are walking by the bongo drum players. Here we pick up the line, *". . . kill us."*, from Mark. So, in terms of scene numbers, we are shooting out of sequence, but in terms of material, we are in sequence—just a different angle of the same scene.

Scene 28
Here we see Ann and Mark part. The surveillance is over.

Scene 33
The street band of musicians put away their instruments. Lunch time is about over and they collect the tips which have been put into the top hat.

Scene 182
This is another angle of the conversation between Ann and Mark. In this walking scene in the square, we can see the anxiety and fear underlining their expressions. This shot could have been done anytime during a scene involving them from Scene 9, where they meet, to Scene 28, where they part.

Scene 185
Again, as we saw in Scene 182, we can hear no dialogue but see that Ann and Mark are talking. This scene could be done anytime the camera is on them from Scene 9 to Scene 28.

Scene 222
Here we find Ann and Mark walking along. They comment on Paul. By checking the script, we find that this is actually 3/4's of Scene 24. But Scene 24 is to be shot from high up giving us a telescopic view. This scene is ground level on Ann and Mark and is shot from a different camera position.

This day we covered 2-4/8 pages. Dealing with the crowd control problem in the square and the staging of these scenes, you have a good, hard Monday scheduled.

DAYS 8 & 9
Tuesday, December 5; Wednesday, December 6

EXT. - Union Square - Eiffel Tower - DAY
EXT. - Office Building Windows - DAY
(10, 11, 25, 26, 17, 31, 18, 23, 24, 103, 32, 13, 30) - 3-2/8
Total - 3-2/8 pages.

Scene 10
Beginning with the lowest scene number first, we find ourselves on the roof of the Eiffel Tower Sign Building. We are looking at Union Square from the POV (Point of View) of the Man On Roof With The Shotgun Microphone, at the people in the Square.

Scene 11
A close-up of Ann talking with Mark.

Scene 25
Man On Roof With Shotgun Microphone scans the people in the square through the telescopic sights on his microphone. He looks for Ann and Mark. (**Note:** Any of the "effects" of looking through a telescopic lens - i.e., cross-hairs, will be added later on. That is an OPTICAL EFFECT which is added in the laboratory.)

Scene 26
Continuation of the Man's POV as he watches Ann and Mark walk past the bongo players. This is another angle of Scene 81

which we scheduled for Day 7 where Mark says the words, *". . . kill us."* In this scene (26), we hear Mark's opening of that line, *"He'd . . . chance"* the rest of which is obliterated by the sound of the bongo drums.

Scene 17
We pan from the man under the Eiffel Tower sign to another man in an office building window.

Scene 31
The surveillance is over. The Man begins to disassemble his shotgun microphone.

This finishes the rooftop sequence. We now move to the Office Building Window where Another Man is tracking Ann and Mark's movements.

Scene 18
This is a POV shot of Ann and Mark and is actually coverage of Scene 68 which we scheduled for Day 5 or 6.

Scene 23
The Man In The Open Window adjusts his microphone sights.

Scene 24
This is a shot of Ann and Mark from the Man In The Open Window's POV. The shot opens with a Close-Up of Ann's face to a TWO-SHOT. Ann comments on seeing Paul. Mark tries to dispell her fears—does all this dialogue sound familiar? This is actually the MASTER SHOT of Scene 71 done from a high angle. In actuality, Scene 71 is Coverage of this scene. Why then, is this the Master Shot? Because, the information which is given in Scene 24 is actually greater than the information in Scene 71 and, on closer inspection, you will also see that Scene 71 is actually only 3/4's of the length of Scene 24.

Scene 103
This is a repeat of part of Scene 24.

Scene 32
The surveillance is over. The Man In The Open Window disassembles his equipment.

Now that all the scenes from the top of the buildings are completed, we shall move back down to the ground and finish the scenes which we have left to do there. Why didn't we schedule this ground work when we were on the ground before? For one reason, many of these shots are close and you wouldn't see all the extras which were needed for the wide shots and high-angle shots of Union Square. Also, since most of the action occurs around the van, we could always have used this as a Cover Set —something which could be shot easily if need be. This is an easily controllable sequence. We shall try to finish the exteriors first.

Scene 13
In this scene, the two Secretaries pass in front of the mirrored panel van and fix their make-up. From the script, we know that Stanley is inside, making comments. Keep in mind that whatever action the secretaries do will have to be repeated on a separate day for the Interior shots, otherwise, the action won't match. We say a separate day, as by now we will probably be running out of light and, therefore, time. If possible, we should try to get this shot quickly and then Scene 30 before we run out of light.

Scene 30
This a simple ESTABLISHING SHOT of the van sitting at the curb. It would be a good idea to have the Second Camera which has been with you doing additional coverage of the scenes set

up their camera for this shot so that as soon as Scene 13 is done and the set is cleared, they can get this shot quickly.

DAY 10
Thursday, December 7

INT. - Paneled Van - DAY
(12, 14-16, 17, 29) 4-4/8
Total - 4-4/8 pages.

All the exterior filming for the Union Square sequence was scheduled first and now, after five days, we are ready to proceed with the Interior of the Paneled Van Truck. If this had been a regular van without any mirrors, we probably wouldn't have scheduled it here. It is essential to the plot, however that we see out the windows onto Union Square.

Scene 12
Beginning with the lowest scene number scheduled for this location, we bring Stanley back to work. He worked on DAY 1 in the park. We have carried him for 8 days (paid him). After today, we will drop him and pick him up later. He is going to be paid for 10 days work although he actually only worked 2. Unfair? Well, if it had been scheduled differently it might have cost a lot more. The importance of scheduling Union Square at this time of the year carries more of a priority than Stanley's Hold Days. If you refer back to your Parameter Factors you will see that Locations are the Number One parameter and Cast is Number Two.

Harry enters the van in this scene. We become aware of his involvement in the recording of Ann and Mark's conversation.

Scenes 14, 15 & 16
Because of the cramped quarters of the Panel Van Truck, these three scenes will probably be shot back to back without really

changing camera positions. We begin with a shot of the secretaries fixing their make-up in front of the mirrors. Then we watch Stanley egg them on in Scene 15, unbeknownst to the secretaries, and then in Scene 16, we discover more about Stanley, Harry and the conversation they are recording. We find out that the equipment they are using is sophisticated and that they are professionals.

Scene 27

As Harry and Stanley continue their surveillance, Paul—dejected at having been discovered by Ann—enters the van, and drops off his recording and surveillance equipment. This scene appears to be simple, but there are actually three actors speaking in addition to Ann and Mark's off-screen lines. The writer/director also mentions seeing the afternoon traffic through the mirrors. This should probably be done as a separate shot or set-up. Because of the cramped conditions, the director may be forced to try for a Master Shot involving all three actors and then go to **OVER-THE-SHOULDER SHOTS** and Close-Ups on each to get his coverage. Confined quarters such as these severely limit movement.

Scene 29

The surveillance is over. The couple has parted. Stanley opens the scene by re-winding the tape recorders. As we have seen in all the UNION SQUARE sequences up to now, there has been a definite "end of surveillance" sequence. The "end of surveillance" sequence begins here with Stanley professionally shutting the operation down while Harry makes a joke.

Judging from the scripted scenes, Ann and Mark really only work in the first scene (Scene 12). Once this scene has been completed, the director will probably allow these two actors to go home for the day. As you progress through the scenes in sequential order, you will find that the need to control the

Exterior (except for excess noise while recording inside the van) will diminish. You are going to cover 4-4/8ths pages today—ambitious but plausible.

This finishes the Union Square location. It took six days to do this work and you completed over 17 pages. Simple division tells you that you are doing almost 3 pages per day. Resist the temptation to generalize like this. Many times, especially in television where schedules are shorter by economic necessity, the production office and/or producer will try to come up with an average page count per day and have the director adhere to it. If you look over the last ten days, you will see that there have been days where we scheduled over 6 pages of work and other days where you were going to be lucky to complete 2/8 of a page. It depends on the material and the other factors needed to shoot the scene. Many times, the shooting of the scene is what takes the least amount of time. It's the getting there, setting up and then packing up that takes the time. You will learn to weigh material and come up with accurate (or more accurate) schedules the more you practice.

Also remember that if you have a first-time director who has not worked with actors before, chances are that it is going to take you longer to complete the work. The director in this instance, *Francis Coppola,* had directed six feature films prior to THE CONVERSATION. His knowledge of the script and his experience with actors were key factors in determining the amount of time each sequence would take to complete.

DAY 11
Friday, December 8
INT. - Amy's Apartment - NIGHT (46, 47) 5-5/8
Total - 5-5/8 pages.

The six days we just completed were all out of doors. Taking the time of year into consideration and the chance of inclement weather (which wouldn't match), it is always a good idea to have a cover set. The Panel Van Truck sequence was one, and this is another. A good cover set is one which can be switched to almost immediately. The Panel Van Truck sequence used the actors which we were already using—Harry, Stanley, Paul (and Ann and Mark). The sequence in Amy's Apartment needs only Harry and Amy. In addition to having the location pre-rigged and pre-lit, we must make arrangements for the actress playing Amy (Teri Garr) to be available not only on this day, but also on any of the other six days we are at Union Square. It is quite important to check the actor's, in this case actress' availability. If you need to call her in earlier than scheduled and have officially placed her on hold so that she cannot accept other employment, you will have to pay her for those days, worked or not.

A cover set such as this can also be used to help stretch the time necessary for a drop and pick-up. This sequence at Amy's apartment lasts for two days. If we found ourselves in a situation where we didn't have enough time between drop and pick-ups on Stanley, Mr. C., or possibly Ann and Mark, this sequence could be slotted into the schedule so that we would have the necessary 10 calendar days.

We begin this location with Scene 46—written as a Night scene. Not knowing what the actual location looks like, whether you can see from the inside that it is night, we have scheduled this location for Friday so that it could possibly be shot at night if need be. Generally, it is easier and less expensive to shoot most night interiors during the day and black out the windows.

In this scene, Harry comes to visit Amy, the girl he keeps. It is his birthday, and he walks in with the bottle of wine which

Mrs. Evangelista gave him. He walks up the staircase (Scene 46) and enters the room (Scene 47). If we had used it as a cover set and some of the scenes needed to be shot at night, we would have re-arranged the order in which they were shot to accommodate the location.

This sequence runs almost six pages. It is also dramatic material between two people. There are no stunts or special effects involved. Since Coppola likes to rehearse his actors before the actual production begins, we are confident that we will be able to finish this material in one day.

DAY 12
Monday, December 11

EXT. - Amy's Apartment - DAY (104) 1/8
INT. - Amy's Apartment Building - DAY (105) 2/8
INT. - Amy's Apartment Bedroom - DAY (106) 1-3/8
INT. - Amy's Apartment Bedroom - DAY (108) 1/8
Total - 1-7/8 pages

Scene 104
It's Monday and we have returned to Amy's apartment. Beginning with the exterior work first. Amy worked in Friday's material. Today involves only Harry.

Scene 105
We move inside to the hallway scene where we observe Harry has abandoned his usually cautious manner. He opens the door.

Scenes 106 & 108
Harry finds that Amy has left him. Ann and Mark's conversation plays back in the background. Whether or not the director wants to use a playback of Ann and Mark's lines is a question

you will have to ask. In order to better control this scene and to place the emphasis on Harry's not finding Amy—and not on Ann and Mark's dialogue, we would suggest using a playback.

All of this dialogue is close to two pages. If things work as planned, this should be a fairly light day and you will complete the location today. You don't have to (and shouldn't try) to kill yourself and your crew every day. It might happen that you didn't finish all of last week's work and had to shoot some of Amy's material today. A light day gives you the opportunity to catch up.

DAY 13
Tuesday - December 12

INT. - Director's Building Elevator - DAY (98, 199, 276–281)
INT. - Dir. Bldg. - Lobby - Newsstand - DAY 366-368) 5/8
Total - 2-3/8 pages.

Scene 98
We go into the elevator of the Director's building. This time it is crowded with people as Harry heads for the penthouse.

Scene 199
Harry is inside the elevator. He is alone. It arrives at the lobby. Since it is supposed to be Sunday, you should make sure to keep the area around the elevator clear.

Scenes 276 - 281
All are taken inside the elevator. As with the Panel Van Truck scenes, shooting in an elevator is difficult and cramped. These five scenes are very short and involve no dialogue at all. While these scenes are being shot, the rest of the crew will be downstairs preparing for the next sequence of shots.

Scenes 366 - 368

Harry looks down at a stack of newspapers. Depending on what the director wants to show in the scene, Scene 367 could be shot as an INSERT—i.e., a shot which is done either earlier or later and inserted in the editing. Holding the important blue pouch in his arms, he walks off toward the elevators.

If we had done this group of shots first, we might have had some crowd control problems as we would have been shooting just as everyone was arriving for work in the elevator. Hopefully, by scheduling this later in the day, we can finish these scenes either before or after everyone who works in the building will need to get in the elevators to go home.

DAY 14
Wednesday, December 13

INT. - Lobby - Director's Office - DAY (200–205) 1 page
INT. - Reception - Director's Office - DAY (273–275) 1-1/8
INT. - Reception - Director's Office - DAY (369–376) 1 page
Total - 3-1/8 pages.

Scenes 200-205

Again, the look should be that of an office on Sunday—empty and quiet. The only thing that may cause any difficulty at all is the dog which is used in Scene 204. Other than that, this sequence should go smoothly. There is no dialogue and not a lot of action.

Scenes 273-275

Now we need to fill in with extras, as this is supposed to be taking place during the week. We introduce the Receptionist who doesn't want Harry to go back to the Director's office.

Scenes 369–376
Practically a repeat of 200 to 205, except that the reception area is crowded with people, including Ann and Mark.

As you can see, we have scheduled the scenes to be done in sequence in a controlled atmosphere. We have gone from the less difficult to the more difficult as we did the day before. In order to make the sequence work effectively, we are going to have to get coverage of Ann and Mark, as well as other actors in this sequence. We are planning to shoot more than three pages today. Until this last sequence, the day should move along very quickly. We will try to finish Scenes 200-205 and 273-275 before lunch so that the afternoon can be spent getting this sequence.

DAY 15
Thursday, December 14
INT. Director's Reception - DAY (Scene 99) 1-4/8
INT. Director's Corridors - DAY (Scene 100 & 102) 5/8
INT. Martin's Office - DAY (Scene 101) 1-1/8
Total - 3-2/8 pages.

As you can see, we are moving toward a specific area—the Director's Office. We are completing scenes within the building complex before moving on to the next area. This is an over-three page day, but most of the work is dialogue between two actors. A new character, Martin (Harrison Ford) begins today. If for any reason we were unable to do the elevator sequences the day before, we would have kept Mr. C. and Martin on alert and used these scenes as a cover set.

DAY 16
Friday, December 15

INT. Director's Office - DAY (206–221) 7-3/8
INT. Director's Office - DAY (223, 224) 4/8
INT. Elevator - DAY (225) 3/8
Total - 8-2/8

We are in the last location inside the Financial Plaza Building: the Director's office. Here, with the exception of the flashback scene (Union Square - 3/8) which we did on Day 7, this entire sequence is played in this office location among the three actors. The page count is 8-2/8 pages—the most we have scheduled so far to be completed in one day. If you had a proper rehearsal period in pre-production, plus a rehearsal the day before, and, if the director is prepared, you should be able to do all this work in one day.

If at all possible, you should always try to get the director to lay out the next day's work if this can be done with a minimum of overtime or any at all on those crew members who should remain after the camera is **WRAPPED** for the day.

We are about to begin the last week before Christmas. Remembering the script, we are going to have a scene in which Harry destroys his apartment looking for a supposed "bug." In order for him to be able to destroy that apartment, a false one will have to be constructed inside. This will take some time. Therefore, we should try to finish all the scenes which take place inside Harry's apartment before that. If we wait until after Christmas to do this, we may not have enough time. Therefore, we should schedule that this week. We have also found out that the location for the attorney's office is only available on Monday. Figuring that we will need at least two days to complete Harry's apartment, that leaves us only with two days before the

Christmas break. Starting any of the large scenes doesn't make any sense. Therefore, we shall fill in the rest of this week with our other small scenes—the Confessional, the Telephone Booth, the Neighborhood Laundry, etc.

DAY 17
Monday, December 18

INT. Lawyer's Office - Brokerage House - DAY (93, 94) 2-3/8
INT. McNaught's Office - DAY (95) 2-7/8
Total - 5-2/8 pages.

Scenes 93, 94
Supposedly representing the apartment tenants, Harry goes to see the attorney, McNaught, to discuss making repairs on the building where he lives. We discover that Harry is secretly the landlord and wants McNaught to stall as he has done in the past. Harry hopes to sell the building to the city.

Scene 95
Harry talks with his niece, Tony, about the problems of growing up. For the first time, we see compassion in his character.

DAY 18
Tuesday, December 19

INT. Harry's Apt. - DAY (40, 41) 1-3/8
Total - 1-3/8 pages

Again, beginning with the lowest scene number, Harry walks into the hallway and checks his mail. He goes into his apartment and, after discovering that Mrs. Evangelista has left a bottle of wine for his birthday, calls her. These two scenes are only 1-3/8 long. Why would we schedule an entire day for this seemingly small amount of work? Well, when you move into a location for the first day, it will take some time in the morning to move your equipment in. From the script we can tell that Harry's apartment is on an upper floor, so you will lose some time having to move equipment up via the stairs and the service elevator. Also, this location will probably not have enough power to operate all the equipment. Therefore, you are going to have to bring in your own generator and run electrical cables. This is not uncommon practice when filming in older buildings. This probably would have happened at Amy's apartment location also.

DAY 19
Wednesday, December 20

INT. Harry's Apt. - NIGHT (42, 43, 44) 5-7/8

Harry is interrupted while cooking his dinner. As you read, you find that the stove he is using is **PRACTICAL**—it actually works. Several of his neighbors join him as they discuss the lack of running water. Harry tries to maneuver the neighbors out of his apartment—but is confronted with a spontaneously provided birthday cake. All this action takes place in Harry's kitchen, living room by the front door and in the hallway. We begin the scene with one actor and end with five. The director may want coverage on them all, which takes time.

DAY 20
Thursday - December 21

EXT. Harry's Apt. - DAY (49) 1/8
INT. Harry's Apt. - NIGHT (48) 3/8
INT. Harry's Apt. - NIGHT (377–379) 3 pages
Total - 3-4/8 pages

Scene 49
When shooting at a location, it is a good idea to try to finish the exteriors before doing the interiors. While you are shooting the exteriors, the crew can be inside finishing up the preparations of the interior. In this instance, it will mean re-dressing the windows for a "night" look.

Scene 48
After finishing Scene 49, we move back inside Harry's apartment for night interiors. As the windows will have been dressed, we will shoot these night interiors during the day time.

Scenes 377, 378, 379
Following this, we can go into the long dialogue sequence between Harry and the tenants, and then Harry talking on the phone with Mark. When we finish these three scenes, we will have completed everything we need to do at Harry's apartment except for the end scenes when he tears the place apart. The Art Department will begin construction on the false walls and floor which Harry will eventually destroy. I would allow at least two weeks for the Art Department to complete their work. Keep in mind that in the real world out there, it is five days before Christmas and everything takes that much longer to do.

DAY 21
Friday, December 22
EXT. Telephone Booth - DAY (92) 1-1/8
INT. Catholic Church - DAY (230, 231) 6/8
INT. Laundry - DAY (39) 5/8
INT. Hotel Auditorium - NIGHT (120, 123, 125) 6/8

Scene 92
The day begins outside in a street telephone booth. If possible, this telephone booth should be set up around the corner from the Catholic Church so as to avoid moving the crew needlessly

and allowing them to finish prepping the Church while this is being shot.

Scenes 230, 231
The company goes to the Catholic Church. Here Harry moves from the church pews to inside the confessional. This sequence should go very quickly as it involves only one actor - Harry.

Scene 39
Harry shows a little boy a magic trick. This scene is in a confined area with three actors. You will probably be dealing with overhead flourescent lights which will have to be replaced as we did in the market. They are the wrong color temperature and will give everything a strange look if not changed. Depending on the number of lights, this should be done before the shooting crew arrives.

Scenes 120 (part), 123, 125
To finish out the day and the week, it makes sense to schedule the three insert shots which will be needed for the St. Francis Hotel Auditorium/Convention. These three shots are actually slides which need to be prepared. Since these scenes involve none of the principal actors, they will be free to go early while still completing a good day's work.

We have now finished our last day of shooting before Christmas. The production company has a choice—either continue shooting during the Holidays, or shut down, let everyone go home and then come back rested and ready to start on Wednesday, January 3. If you are faced with having to shoot around Christmas time, if at all possible, try to arrange your schedule so that you will be able to give your crew some time off. Most everyone will go off salary during that time, although you will still have some overhead costs to maintain. Your crew should be rested and ready to begin the second half of the picture. The period between Christmas and New Year's is usually the least productive period during the year. If you can avoid shooting during this time, you should. In the instance of "The Conversation," the crew elected to go off payroll and take the time off.

DAY 22
Wednesday, January 3

EXT. Continental Lodge - DAY (232–236) 5/8
INT. Continental Lodge Lobby - DAY (237) 3/8
INT. Continental Lodge Corridor - DAY (238) 2/8
INT. Continental Lodge Corridor - DAY (254) 1/8
Total - 1-3/8 pages

A new year and a new location. We go to the Continental Lodge. Again, follow the exteriors first rule and try to keep in sequential order.

Scenes 232-236
Scene 232 is actually a second unit shot as it involves no principal actors. But since it doesn't make sense to send a Second Unit back here to get a quick 1/8 of a page shot of the motel sign, we shall do this shot before we ask Harry to be on the set. Scenes 233–236 are either of Harry or are Harry's POV of the motel. Harry's POV shots will be scheduled and shot first, and then Harry will be called on to the set to shoot the other scenes.

Scene 237
Harry walks in and asks for a particular room. This involves dialogue and two actors and shouldn't take much time to shoot.

Scene 238
Harry arrives at his room and enters.

Scene 254
This corridor scene needs to be shot at night. Depending on which motel has been chosen, it is possible that the corridor is

outside which would make shooting day-for-night difficult at best. Hopefully, because we are shooting in winter and it gets dark very early, we will be able to get this night shot without having to stay too long. Otherwise, we may have to create the illusion of night time.

Remembering that you have now had almost ten days off, it would be a good idea, if time allows, to block and rehearse the following day's work which has Harry entering the motel room. It's also possible that the crew would have time to pre-light the room.

DAY 23
Thursday, January 4

INT. Cont. Lodge Bedroom B-5 - DAY (239, 240) 2/8
INT. Cont. Lodge Bathroom B-5 - DAY (241–244) 1-1/8
INT. Cont. Lodge Bedroom B-5 DAY (245–250) 1 page
INT. Cont. Lodge Bedroom B-5 - NIGHT (251–253) 3/8
Total - 2-6/8 pages

You will note that the bedroom and bathroom scenes can be scheduled together as one location. The way it lays out in the script, you go from bedroom to bathroom and then back to the bedroom. This could be considered a double move (back to the bedroom). Actually, the whole motel room is one set. The bathrooms of most motels are small and require little preparation time (changing and setting some lights). Harry checks out the room and his neighbors in B-7 by going out onto his little terrace. In the bathroom, he begins to eavesdrop on the conversation next door. He believes that he hears Mr. C. killing Ann and Mark. In terror, he runs and hides under the bedcovers and turns the TV on to block out the murderous screams. He awakens at night and turns off the TV. Despite the fact that this scene requires only one actor and no dialogue, it will take some time because your action takes place within three specific areas in the motel room. Your director will probably want a lot of coverage to be able to create suspense. Most likely, the first three scenes will be scheduled and finished as it gets dark so that the Night Bedroom scene can be shot. Otherwise, the room windows will have to be dressed for night.

DAY 24
Friday, January 5

INT. Cont. Lodge Bedroom B-7 - NIGHT (255–260) - 1 page
INT. Cont. Lodge Bathroom B-7 - NIGHT (261–268) 1-3/8
EXT. Cont. Lodge - NIGHT (270) - 1/8
INT. Cont. Lodge Bathroom - NIGHT - (354) 1/8
INT. Cont. Lodge Bedroom - NIGHT - (269) 1/8
Total - 2-6/8 pages.

As this is a Friday, we can shoot all these scenes night-for-night as they are written, finish late and not worry about shooting early on Saturday. The crew's next call will be for Monday.

Scenes 255–260, 261–268, 270, 354, 269
Harry walks through the immaculately cleaned motel room. He finally discovers the clogged toilet which backs up—spilling bloody water onto the tile floor and then onto his shoes. The toilet backing up is a Special Effects shot which will have to be set up before hand. Although the page count for this day is only 2-6/8 pages, we are shooting at night, have many set-ups and some special effects work. This will be a good night's work.

DAY 25
Monday, January 8

INT. Cont. Lodge - Bedroom B-7 - DAY (363) 2/8
INT. Cont. Lodge - Bedroom B-7 - DAY (359–361) 1 page

INT. Cont. Lodge - Bathroom B-7 - DAY (356) 4/8
Total - 1-6/8 pages

You will notice right away that we have not scheduled these
scenes to be shot in sequential order. Why? The nature of the
scenes make it better for us to start with a clean set and then
get bloody. In reality, after reading these scenes, you will see
that although this shooting order is not chronological, it actually is in the correct time order. Mr. C. plays the tape for Ann
and Mark. Next, Mark locks the door. They do this before they
stab him. Then we see Ann and Mark stab Mr. C. in Scenes
359–361 and then, finally in Scene 356, we see them cleaning
up the blood as Mr. C. lies dead. Coppola purposely juxtaposed
the scenes to give you the impression that you are "seeing"
what happened in the room through Harry's interpretation of
the taped conversation.

When we finish today's work, we will have finished Mr. C. and
Mark's work for the picture. Look back over your schedule.
The last day that we used Mark was (Day 15) and the last day
we used Mr. C. was (Day 16). Now count the days off (including the Christmas vacation). As you can see, enough time
lapsed between their last day's work and this so that we could
drop and pick up both the actors. So as not to have any actors
waiting to work, it would be advisable to see if we can complete
Ann's work as soon as possible. Both Stanley and Paul were
dropped on Day 10 and won't be picked up until later in the
schedule.

DAYS 26 & 27
Tuesday, January 9 & Wednesday, January 10

EXT/INT - Bus - DAY (284, 285, 289, 291) 4/8
INT. Bus - DAY (298, 300, 301, 302) 1-3/8
EXT. Bus - LATE DAY (299) 1/8

EXT. Bus - NIGHT (303, 304) 2/8
INT. Bus - NIGHT (305, 306) 1-6/8
EXT. Bus and Street - NIGHT (307, 308) 3/8
INT. Bus & Street - DAY (287, 288, 292, 293, 295, 296) 7/8
EXT. Poles and Lines (Inserts) - DAY (286, 290, 294) 3/8
EXT. Street & Harry's Bus - DAY (297) 1/8
Total - 5-6/8 pages

Look back at your schedule. On Day 4 we had Ann and Harry
on the Electric Buses then. Why didn't we continue with them?
Read closely and you will see that the scene is not really taking
place on the bus. Harry follows Ann as she walks from the
Plaza and boards a bus and then he boards one behind. We
really don't get inside the bus with Ann and Harry. Harry has
also been in buses on Day 2 and on Day 3. We really have to
look at the Electric Bus sequences as separate locations. The
main scheduling problem is to finish the Union Square sequence
in time so that the sound tapes are ready to playback in the
Warehouse sequence. The few short Electric Bus scenes which
we scheduled earlier fit into the schedule and were not difficult
to do. This sequence, however, is going to take us at least two
days to shoot.

We begin this sequence in the daytime, move into the late
afternoon and continue into the evening. Looking at the material you have left to schedule, you can see that we are going to
be in for a few evenings of night shooting. The change from day
to night occurs in Scene 303 with an Exterior Shot of the Bus
in which they are riding. After reading over the material, you
realize that this is a lot of material to cover which requires
much action and a dramatic conflict between the two main
actors. Harry is going to be jumping in and out of buses—
running from one to another. Because of the added difficulties
of shooting at night, we have scheduled this over two days

105

(nights). We shall continue with the night work so that we can finish Ann. What will happen most likely is that we will begin shooting the day/late day sequences, finish some of the night work, return the next day late in the afternoon with Harry alone to do his scenes (beginning with Scene 287), do the inserts and then Scene 297 making this second day a fairly short day/night.

DAY 28
Thursday, January 11

EXT. Stepped Street - NIGHT (309–316) 1-1/8
EXT. The Park - NIGHT (317–332) 4-3/8
Total - 5-4/8 pages

Scenes 309–316
We see Harry pursuing Ann down the streets. It makes most sense to begin with Ann's scenes first and shoot all of hers, and then begin the SINGLES on Harry. This is the director's decision, so we are leaving the option up to him. This night's work could be shot with a hand-held camera.

Scenes 317–332
Harry follows Ann into a multi-level park. He pours out his innermost feelings to her in an effort to purge his guilt. Together, these two sequences are 5-4/8 pages long. Why do we think that we can do this in one night when the same amount of material took two days' before (Tuesday & Wednesday)? Well, first you have very little dialogue. From Scene 309 on to Scene 332, Ann has one line of dialogue, *"Please leave me alone."* Harry does all the talking. Secondly, you have very few locations involved. The main location is in the park and Harry walks along the first level delivering his lines, ending up sitting on a small bench. If the actors have been able to rehearse the

scene in pre-production, then we should be able to accomplish this work in one night.

When we do, Ann will have completed all her work on this picture and be done.

DAY 29
Friday, January 12

INT. Harry's Apartment - NIGHT (380–397) 2-7/8
Total - 2-7/8 pages.

The Art Department and Construction Department should have had enough time to re-dress this apartment and construct the false walls and floor which Harry will rip out. It is one thing to take a telephone apart or remove an electrical wall plate, and entirely another to steam off wall paper and pull up the wooden floor. In the script, Harry does not tear into the walls or the floor. Francis Coppola decided that it would be a good idea to convey the character's total desperation and helplessness. After reading the 2-7/8 pages, it becomes obvious that it would take an entire day (or night) of shooting to get all the necessary shots for this sequence. If this isn't planned properly, it will take longer. Since this is a night sequence and since you are on location with windows which could look out to the world, it should be scheduled at night.

DAYS 30 & 31
Monday, January 13 & Tuesday, January 14

EXT. Harry's Warehouse - DAY (50) 2/8
INT. Harry's Warehouse - DAY (51–57, 59–61, 63, 65, 67, 69, 70, 72–80, 82–86, 88–91) 11-6/8
Total - 9-3/8 pages

As we now begin our seventh week, you can see that we have established a clear pattern of grouping our day work and our night work and trying to shoot in sequential order at a location. We try to schedule all the night work for the latter part of the week. This week we are going to begin the Harry's Warehouse sequence. This is a classic example of good scheduling by Clark Paylow, the production manager on THE CONVERSATION. Harry's warehouse is, most likely, an actual location and not a built set. It will probably be a large warehouse with large windows made of safety glass. Unless there is an area within the warehouse which can be shielded from the windows, you are going to feel as if you are shooting in a fishbowl and will be at the mercy of the sun. You will probably have to shoot what is called for in the script—day-for-day and night-for-night without faking it.

Scene 50
Harry walks along the exterior of his place of business. This is the first and only time we see the Warehouse exterior in the day time.

Scenes 51–57
We move inside to where Harry begins analyzing his tapes.

Scenes 59–61
We see Harry operate the recording equipment professionally. This is very easy to say, but will require many hours of rehearsal time which shall have to be scheduled most likely during pre-production. We will need to have copies of the conversation which Harry taped in Union Square to play back during these scenes. Stanley is now in these scenes. We pick him up again after dropping him on Day 10.

Scene 63, 65, 67
Trying to shoot in sequential order as much as possible because of the potential light problem, we now schedule the disagree-

ment between Stanley and Harry. Stanley leaves for lunch in a huff. Harry continues to work.

Scenes 69, 70, 72–80
Alone, Harry continues to work on the tapes. We watch him as he professionally works the dials and switches. He uses some of his homemade equipment to further decipher the tapes.

Scenes 82–86
Harry checks the results. He has filtered out most of the static and has added more meaning to their conversation.

Scenes 88–91
Harry pushes the rewind button, looks at the tape and then at the still photographs of Ann and Mark.

By finishing this sequence, we have completed 11-3/8 pages of work in two days. As you can see from the scenes, we are doing a lot of coverage of the equipment working. Also, we have now completed all the daytime work at this location and shall move into three day's of night work.

DAYS 32, 33, & 34
Wednesday, January 15; Thursday, January 16, Friday January 17.
INT. Harry's Warehouse - NIGHT (160–173) 19-4/8

This sequence begins with a dark warehouse and then the group from the St. Francis Hotel arriving for the impromptu party. In the next thirteen scenes, you have seven actors working. Once we begin these actors, we will concentrate on keeping their schedules tight so that we can finish them quickly. More than five pages of this entire sequence involves Harry and Meredith dancing and talking (Scenes 161–164). Approximately seven pages involves Harry and Moran engaged in conversation with most of the others joining in (Scenes 164–173). This part of the sequence occurs in and out of the caged area where Harry keeps his personal equipment. We are looking at shooting an entire sequence which runs 19-4/8 pages. It should be obvious that we cannot attempt this in one or even two days. With a rehearsal and time to block the action beforehand, we should be able to finish this in three long, hard days. If we run into any problems, we can always go into a fourth day.

DAYS 35 & 36
Monday, January 20; Tuesday, January 21

INT. Harry's Warehouse - NIGHT (174–181, 183–184, 186, 187) 10-6/8
Total - 10-6/8 pages

We continue shooting night for night. We continue where we left off with Harry and Meredith. The others have left the party and now Harry and Meredith continue talking. Judging from the page count (10-6/8 pages), the movement within the warehouse, and the amount of dialogue between the two, this is going to require two day's (night's) work.

DAY 37
Wednesday, January 22

INT. Harry's Warehouse - NIGHT (337–353, 355, 357–358, 362, 364) 4-6/8
EXT. Harry's Warehouse - NIGHT (333–336) 4/8
Total - 5-2/8 pages

Why are we breaking rules—shooting out of sequence and not shooting the exteriors first? Since we are already set up inside, to stop now and shoot exteriors would mean moving all the equipment outside, only to move it back inside again. We don't need to have a double move. Plus, while we are finishing up inside, the rest of the crew can be setting up lights for the exteriors.

After completing the interior work which is the major portion of the work (5-4/8 pages), we can begin to partially STRIKE the inside set (location), removing any equipment which we will not need. If the ceiling is pre-rigged, then the equipment should not be removed until after the DAILIES have been seen and approved.

Harry discovers that someone is breaking into his warehouse as he arrives. He scares the burglars away. Before they leave, they turn on his tape recorder. Harry listens to the tape again and discovers a new meaning to Ann's line, *"Do you think we can do it?"*

From Harry's point of view (POV) he sees two men. We don't actually see them. The majority of tonight's work is on Harry. We should be able to finish it in one night.

DAY 38
Thursday, January 23

INT. - Staff Car - NIGHT (Scenes 144, 146 - 6/8)
INT/EXT. - Staff Car - NIGHT (Scenes 147, 148 - 2/8)
INT/EXT. - Staff Car - NIGHT (Scene 149 - 3/8)
INT. - Staff Car - NIGHT (Scenes 151, 152, 153, 155 - 6/8)
INT. - Staff Car - NIGHT (Scenes 157, 158 - 2/8)
INT. - Staff Car - NIGHT (Scene 159- 1/8)

EXT. - Street/Mustang - NIGHT (Scenes 145, 150, 154, 156
- 4/8)
Total - 3 pages

Properly planned, this night driving sequence can be finished in
one evening. Through careful reading, it is a driving and dialogue sequence, not a stunt/chase sequence. Only one time does
the driver of the Mustang almost lose control of this car (Scene
150 - Stunt). The Mustang Driver has only one line which he
delivers while sitting at a stop light. Therefore, you are placing
your emphasis on the Staff Car. In order to cut down on the
time needed to make the vehicle ready for filming (installing
FRONT and **SIDE CAR MOUNTS** for the camera, and possibly a
battery pack in the trunk to provide power for the lights needed
to shoot the interior of the car) you should have more than one
car available. The duplicate Staff Car could be pre-rigged with
car mounts—special devices which hold the 35mm camera on
a platform—in place. Other mounts, then, are used to hold the
lights inside the car. These car mounts can be put on any
number of places on the car. The most common placement is
on the side of the car and on the hood. We explain this to you
now because most of this sequence will be shot with the use of
car mounts. In addition to the platforms, a **CAMERA CAR** will
probably also be used as well as **RUN-BYS** (shots of the car
driving by a stationary camera). To play it safe, it would be a
good idea to duplicate the Mustang, too. If anything should
happen to either vehicle (mechanical failure, accident, etc.) you
wouldn't lose any time. When you are spending well over
$70,000 per night for night shooting, a stand-by car is inexpen-
sive insurance. You might find that this material should be shot
using **PROCESS SHOTS.** The car itself would be placed on a
sound stage and film of a moving background would be projected onto a transparent screen behind. In this case, the director chose to shoot everything on location.

DAY 39
Friday, January 24

INT. Hotel Convention Bar - NIGHT (133–136) - 1-5/8
INT. Hotel Convention - NIGHT (137–142) 4-3/8
EXT. Hotel Convention - NIGHT (143) 6/8
Total - 6-6/8 pages

Since Thursday was a night call, we must continue with, at best, a late afternoon crew call.

Scenes 133–136
Harry tries to make a phone call, hangs up and runs into Martin from Mr. C's office.

Scenes 137–142
We pick up Harry, inside the convention center, being hustled over to Moran's booth. Moran has placed a bug in the Ladies' room and they are all eavesdropping. Meredith and Lurleen join the boys as they head for the door. This sequence has two key filming areas—by Moran's booth and by the Ladies' room. In the rehearsal period and on the location scout, this scene should be laid out and blocked in advance.

Scene 143
If you were able to give your crew a late afternoon call, then it is probably dark enough outside to do the Parking Lot scene. Although it is Friday night and everyone is tired after almost 1-1/2 weeks of night shooting, we are going to try to finish this scene tonight. It isn't too long or very difficult. Here you will be able to control the vehicle and pedestrian traffic outside in the hotel parking lot. Once you get the Master Shot of all of them trying to get into the car and, possibly, driving off, the

coverage should be fairly easy to control. While you were inside doing the previous scenes, part of your crew should be out here setting up for this scene. It should be obvious to you that we did our interiors here first so that we could finish Friday evening with a night exterior.

DAY 40
Monday, January 27

INT. Hotel Convention - NIGHT (109–120-part) 2-3/8
INT. Hotel Auditorium - NIGHT (121–122, 124) 1-5/8
Total - 4 pages

Scenes 109–120-part
Having completed the night exterior on Friday, we can go back to sequential shooting beginning with the first scene scheduled for this location. Depending on the location and the amount of daylight you actually see from the convention room, you should be able to shoot this day-for-night.

The opening sequence establishes the convention. With the number of extras you are going to have, it will take longer to shoot this sequence. We bring back Martin. He is at the Convention to see Harry.

Scenes 121, 122, 124
Having scheduled and completed part of Scene 120 as well as Scenes 123 and 125 on Day 21, the slide show presentation coverage is already done. That leaves us to focus on Harry entering the auditorium and looking around. Your extras are watching the activity, so there shouldn't be too much coordination. Paul greets Harry.

114

DAY 41
Tuesday, January 28

INT. Hotel Convention Center - Main Room - NIGHT (126–132) 8-7/8

Harry and Paul enter the main room where the exhibit booths are located. Harry, Moran, and Meredith meet. This is a long sequence—almost nine pages long, but over half of it involves Moran giving a stand-up demonstration of his surveillance device. Harry moves on and discusses equipment with another dealer from Elco Electronics. These two areas within the main convention center room should be rehearsed and blocked. The result would be being able to complete close to seven pages in this, the last day of shooting.

One last bit of advice before moving onto the shooting schedule, if at all possible when working on a production as a production manager or first assistant director, try always to get your director to lay out the next day's work if it can be done with a minimum of overtime, or any at all, on those crew members who should remain after the camera is wrapped for the day. This will help immeasurably when you find yourself up against a tight schedule.

Well, congratulate yourself. You have just made it through the breakdown and scheduling of a feature film. Study the Production Board. Make sure you understand the reasons THE CONVERSATION was scheduled this way. I hope that many of you have gone along and prepared your own color-coded board as an exercise. As I stressed before, the best way to learn how to schedule a film is to do it!

IX

THE SHOOTING SCHEDULE

A SHOOTING SCHEDULE is another production board, only typed on a form. Sometimes only a little information is listed, sometimes more. The schedule will be handed out to all the cast and crew. Revisions of the shooting schedule should be handed out just as soon as they are available. Using a different color paper and dating the sheets will make it easy to know which is the most current. The schedule will give the cast and crew a projection of how the show is laid out and when certain scenes have been scheduled.

In order to make sure that all pertinent information is listed on the shooting schedule, it is a good idea to go over the breakdown sheet and see what else should be included. Special equipment, wardrobe, stunt doubles, etc., which might not appear on the production strip board due to lack of space are on the breakdown sheets and should appear on the shooting schedule. Also, have your marked up script handy to double-check any last minute questions which might arise.

Now, please turn to the Shooting Schedule on the following pages.

SHOOTING SCHEDULE

FRANCIS FORD COPPOLA PRODS.

TITLE: **THE CONVERSATION**   PRODUCERS: F. F. COPPOLA
                                          F. ROOS
                                          M. SKAGER
SHOOTING DATES: 11/26/-- THRU
                1/30/--   DIRECTOR: F. F. COPPOLA
                           PROD. MGR: CLARK PAYLOW
                           ASST. DIR. C. MYERS
TOTAL PAGES: 157

DAY/DATE	SET/SCENES	CAST/ATMOS	STAGE/LOCATION
DAY 1 SUNDAY 11/26/--	**EXT. FINANCIAL DISTRICT (SUNDAY) (D)** Scenes: 195-198 5/8 Harry through Sunday Streets, signs in goes up.	#1 - HARRY EXTRAS: Uniformed Sec. Guard	#1 EMBARCADERO BUILDING PROPS Blue Pouch Gun For Guard Clipboard

DAY/DATE	SET/SCENES	CAST/ATMOS	STAGE/LOCATION
DAY 1 cont'd.	**EXT. FINANCIAL DIST. (PHONE BOOTH) (D)**	#1 - HARRY	PROPS Blue Pouch (Empty)
	Scenes: 226-229 4/8		
	Harry at loose ends, gets into phone booth.		
	COMPANY MOVES TO GOLDEN GATE PARK (BANDSTAND AREA)		
	EXT. GOLDEN GATE PARK (D)	#1 - HARRY #5 - STAN	EXT. G/G PARK
	Scenes: 188-194 2-3/8	EXTRAS Old Woman in Park	PROPS Blue Pouch
	Harry accosts Stan. Tells him that Meredith has gone through his things. Tells him to stay away from him.	MEN IN SUITS TO PASS OUT PROGRAMS. GEN. ATMOS.	MUSIC BAND
	END OF FIRST DAY		

119

DAY/DATE	SET/SCENES	CAST/ATMOS	STAGE/LOCATION
DAY 2 MONDAY 11/27/--	**EXT. STREET/ELECT. BUS/NEIGHBORHOOD (D)**	#1 - HARRY	FILLMORE & HAYES STREET - YOUNG'S FOOD MART
6/8	Scene 34, 36, 37 3/8	EXTRAS Bus Driver #1	EFX Sparks from Bus.
	Scene 34 - Electric Bus travels up street (1/8)	Atmos. on Bus.	
	Scene 36 - Driver fixes rod, Harry walks toward his home. (1/8)		
	Scene 37 - Bus passes Harry. (1/8)		

DAY/DATE	SET/SCENES	CAST/ATMOS	STAGE/LOCATION
DAY 2 cont'd.	**INT. ELECT. BUS (D)** Scene 35 2/8 Harry on bus. driver off to fix rod. Harry gets off	EXTRAS Bus Driver #1 Atmos. on Bus	PROPS Packages, Brief-cases, etc. for passengers.
	INT. MARKET (D) Scene 38 1/8th Harry shops.	#1 - HARRY EXTRAS Counter Man (clerk) Others, if needed.	PROPS Tomato, Pork Chops (in cellophane), can of beer, money, sack/purchases.

END OF SECOND DAY

DAY/DATE	SET/SCENES	CAST/ATMOS	STAGE/LOCATION
DAY 3 TUESDAY 11/28/-- 2/8	**EXT. STREET (D)** (Burning Car) Scene 365 1/8 Mr. C and car go up up in flames	#4 - MR. C (Stunt Dbl?)	PROPS Blood on Mr. C. EFX Car Burns
	INT./EXT. ELECT. BUS & STREET (N) Scene 45 1/8 Harry w/wine on bus.	#1 - HARRY EXTRAS Bus Driver #2 Few atmos. on bus.	LOCATION #2 PROPS Bottle/Wine

END OF THIRD DAY

122

DAY/DATE	SET/SCENES	CAST/ATMOS	STAGE/LOCATION
DAY 4 WEDNESDAY 11/29/--	**EXT. FINANCIAL DISTRICT (D)**	#1 - HARRY	SANSOME & CALIF. STREETS
7/8	Scenes 96, 97 2/8	EXTRAS Gen. atmos on street (25)	PROPS Blue Pouch
	Harry heads for Mr. C.'s office.		
	EXT. FINANCIAL PLAZA (D)	#1 - HARRY	PROPS Attache Case
	Scenes 272, 272 2/8	EXTRAS Atmos.(75)	
	Harry heads through work day crowds for Mr. C.		
	COMPANY MOVES TO #1 EMBARCADERO - CLAY ST. ALCOA PLAZA		

DAY/DATE	SET/SCENES	CAST/ATMOS	STAGE/LOCATION
DAY 4 cont'd.	**EXT. DIRECTOR'S BLDG. (BUS #1 & #2)** **(D)**	#1 - HARRY #2 - ANN #37-DRIVER (Bus #1) #38-DRIVER (Bus #2)	#1 EMBARCADERO CLAY ST/ALCOA PL.
		EXTRAS Passengers on both buses.	PROPS 2 Elect. Trolleys Attache Case
	Scenes 282, 283 3/8 Ann gets onto bus, Harry follow on second bus.		EFX Fog?

END OF FOURTH DAY

DAY/DATE	SET/SCENES	CAST/ATMOS	STAGE/LOCATION
DAYS 5&6 THURSDAY 11/30-- FRIDAY, 12/1/-- 6-7/8	**EXT. UNION SQUARE (D)** Scenes 1-9, 3-1/8th Establishes Union Square. Harry drinks coffee & watches Ann and Mark talk. Harry moves from bench to van. Pan to Man w/ microphone on top of City of Paris Bldg.	# 1 - HARRY # 2 - ANN # 3 - MARK #6 - PAUL #21 - MIME #22 - YNG MAN #23 - YNG WOM ST. ATMOS Derelict Eiffel Tower Man Street Band	UNION SQUARE PROPS Lunch for Mark Coffee in sack for Harry Mirror van w/sign "Bay Cities Glass & Mirror Co." Shotgun Microphone w/telescopic sight Earphones Paper Bag and Hearing Aid-Paul MUSIC Street Band - "Red Red Robin."

DAY/DATE	SET/SCENES	CAST/ATMOS	STAGE/LOCATION
DAYS 5 & 6 cont'd	**EXT. UNION SQ. (D) (FTG FOR WRHSE. SEQ.)**	# 2 - ANN # 3 - MARK # 6 - PAUL #21 - MIME	PROPS Lunch Sack Mirror Van Sack & Hearing Aid
	Scenes: 58, 62, 64, 66, 68, 71, 87, 107 3-4/8		
		EXTRAS Derelict Street Band	MUSIC Red Red Robin
	Scene 58 (5/8) Fragment conv. Mark/Ann		
	Scene 62 (3/8) Mark & Ann talk about gift.	ATMOS Gen. Street.	NOTE Repeat footage sequences
	Scene 64 (1/8) View of Derelict.		

DAY/DATE	SET/SCENES	CAST/ATMOS	STAGE/LOCATION
DAYS 5 & 6 cont'd.	Scene 66 (3/8) Ann & Mark walk past derelict.		
	Scene 68 (7/8) Ann & Mark talk – Mime.		
	Scene 71 (4/8) Ann spots Paul.		
	Scene 87 (4/8) Ann & Mark kiss goodbye.		
	Scene 107 (1/8) Ann & Mark kiss goodbye.		
END OF FIFTH & SIXTH DAYS -- END OF FIRST WEEK			

DAY/DATE	SET/SCENES	CAST/ATMOS	STAGE/LOCATION
DAY 7 MONDAY 12/4/-- 2-4/8	**EXT. UNION SQ. (D)** Scenes 19-22 1-1/8 Ann & Mark continue walking. Paul trails behind; they spot him. He leaves.	#2 - ANN #3 - MARK #6 - PAUL #21 - MIME #24 - SHOPPER #1 #25 - SHOPPER #2 #26 - SHOPPER #3 EXTRAS Street Atmos.	UNION SQUARE PROPS Lunch Bag Paper Bag Hearing Aid Hearing Aid
	EXT. UNION SQ. (D) Scene 81 3/8 Mark's voice distorts, "kill us."	#2 - ANN #3 - MARK EXTRAS Bongo Players Street Atmos.	MUSIC Red Red Robin

DAY/DATE	SET/SCENES	CAST/ATMOS	STAGE/LOCATION
DAY 7 cont'd.	**EXT. UNION SQ. (D)**	# 2 - ANN # 3 - MARK #21 - MIME	MUSIC Red, Red Robin
	Scenes 28, 33 3/8		
		EXTRAS Derelict Street Atmos. (thinning out)	PROPS Lunch sack/Mark
	Scene 28 (2/8) Ann & part company. Derelict awakens, Mark throws away sack & leaves.		
	Scene 33 (1/8) - Musicians pack up.		

129

DAY/DATE	SET/SCENES	CAST/ATMOS	STAGE/LOCATION
DAY 7 cont'd.	**EXT. UNION SQ. (D)** **(SUPER O/WHSE SEQ.)**	# 2 - ANN # 3 - MARK #21 - MIME	PROPS Lunch sack/Mark
	Scenes 182, 185 2/8	EXTRAS Derelict Street Band Atmos.	MUSIC Red, Red Robin
	Scene 182 (1/8) Mark and Ann circle park.		
	Scene 184 (1/8) Pan of terrified Ann through park.		

130

DAY/DATE	SET/SCENES	CAST/ATMOS	STAGE/LOCATION
DAY 7 cont'd.	**EXT. UNION SQ. (D)** (PREVIOUS FOOTAGE) Scene 222 (3/8)	# 2 - ANN # 3 - MARK # 6 - PAUL #21 - MIME	PROPS Paper sack/Paul Lunch/Mark
	Ann and Mark spot Paul.	EXTRAS Derelict Street Band	MUSIC
	END OF SEVENTH DAY		

DAY/DATE	SET/SCENES	CAST/ATMOS	STAGE/LOCATION
DAYS 8&9 TUESDAY 12/5/-- BLDG.	**EXT. EIFFEL TOWER** **ROOF - (D)**	# 2 - ANN # 3 - MARK # 6 - PAUL	UNION SQUARE CITY OF PARIS PROPS Shotgun Microphone w/ earphones Nylon Bag Mirror Van Lunch/Mark Bag/Paul Bongo drums.
WEDNESDAY 12/6/-- 3-2/8	Scenes 10, 11, 25, 26, 17, 31 1-3/8 Scenes 10, 11 (3/8) Man's POV - Ann & Mark talking. Scene 25 (1/8) Man tracks Ann & Mark with microphone. Scene 26 (4/8) - Tele POV Ann & Mark near bongos.	EXTRAS Man on Roof #1 Derelict Atmos. in Sq. Street Band	

continued....

DAY/DATE	SET/SCENES	CAST/ATMOS	STAGE/LOCATION
DAYS 8&9 cont'd.	**EXT. EIFFEL TOWER** **ROOF – (D)**		
	Scene 17 (2/8) – Pan from Man #1 to Man #2. Scene 31 (1/8) – Man #1 disassembles microphone & puts in bag.		
	EXT. TOP OF BLDG. **WINDOW & SQUARE – (D)**	# 2 – ANN # 3 – MARK # 6 – PAUL #21 – MIME	UNION SQUARE
	Scenes 18, 23, 24, 103, 32. 1-5/8	EXTRAS Man #2 Derelict St. Atmos. Street Band	PROPS Shotgun Microphone Lunch Sack/Mark Mirror Van Paper Bag/Paul
	Scenes 18, 23 – Man tracks couple (3/8)		
	Scenes 24, 103 – Tele POV of Ann & Mark spotting Paul (1-1/8)		NOTE Repeated footage
	Scene 32 (1/8) – Man packs gear & puts away.		

133

DAY/DATE	SET/SCENES	CAST/ATMOS	STAGE/LOCATION
DAYS 8&9 cont'd.	**EXT. VAN - UNION SQ. (D)** Scenes 13, 30 (2/8) Scene 13 - (1/8) Secretaries primp in front of mirror on van. Scene 30 - (1/8) Van w/ laughing within.	<u>EXTRAS</u> 2 Secretaries Str. Atmos.	UNION SQUARE <u>PROPS</u> Mirror Van

END OF EIGHTH AND NINTH DAYS

DAY/DATE	SET/SCENES	CAST/ATMOS	STAGE/LOCATION
DAY 10 THURSDAY 12/7/-- 4-4/8	**INT. MIRROR VAN (D)** Scene 12 4/8 Stan watching tapes. Harry enters, takes up surveillance w/ binoculars.	# 1 - HARRY # 5 - STAN EXTRAS Atmos Outside	UNION SQUARE OR COVER SET PROPS Eyeglasses Binoculars Coffee
	INT. MIRROR VAN (D) Scenes 14, 15, 16. 2-1/8 Harry watches, Stan takes photos of the secretaries. Harry tells him to get back to work. Stan wonders who they are working for. They check reception.	# 1 - HARRY # 5 - STAN EXTRAS Secretaries St. Atmos.	UNION SQUARE OR COVER SET PROPS Binoculars Coffee Motorized Nikon Mirror Van

135

DAY/DATE	SET/SCENES	CAST/ATMOS	STAGE/LOCATION
DAY 10 cont'd.	**INT. MIRROR VAN (D)**	# 1 - HARRY # 5 - STAN # 6 - PAUL	UNION SQUARE
	Scenes 27, 29. 1-7/8		PROPS Headset Coffee Shopping Bag Electronic Device Hearing Aid. Money/Billfold
	Scene 27 - Paul comes into van, says he's been spotted. Harry pays him, thanks him and Paul leaves. (1-2/8)	EXTRAS St. Atmos	
	Scene 29 - Stan & Harry start to wrap it up. Harry makes a joke "mind your own business." (5/8)		

END OF THE TENTH DAY

DAY/DATE	SET/SCENES	CAST/ATMOS	STAGE/LOCATION
DAY 11 FRIDAY 12/8/-- 5-5/8	**INT. AMY'S APT. BUILDING (N)** Scene 46 2/8 Harry goes to apt. Lets himself in.	# 1 - HARRY #16 - AMY (os)	116 FREDERICKSON #114. <u>PROPS</u> Wine DoorKey
	INT. AMY'S APT. (N) Scene 47 5-3/8 Harry tells Amy it's his b'day. They toast. Amy asks questions... Harry cuts her off. She hums song which disturbs him. He leaves her money for rent and goes.	# 1 - HARRY #16 - AMY	116 FREDERICKSON #114 <u>PROPS</u> Wine bottle Stereo Photos on walls Rent money Wine glasses Opener

END OF ELEVENTH DAY - END OF SECOND WEEK

DAY/DATE	SET/SCENES	CAST/ATMOS	STAGE/LOCATION
DAY 12 MONDAY 12/11/--	**EXT. AMY'S BLDG (D)**	#1 - HARRY	116 FREDERICKSON #114
	Scene 104 1/8th		<u>PROPS</u> Pouch Key
1-7/8	Harry rushes to Amy's.		
	INT. AMY'S APT (D)	#1 - HARRY	116 FREDERICKSON #114
	Scenes 105, 106, 108 1-6/8		<u>PROPS</u> Pouch Money in Saucer
	Amy is gone, rent money untouched. Mark & Ann's conversation plays o.s. Harry is alone, upset.		

END OF TWELFTH DAY

DAY/DATE	SET/SCENES	CAST/ATMOS	STAGE/LOCATION
DAY 13 TUESDAY 12/12/-- 2-3/8	**INT. MR.C'S BLDG. ELEVATOR (D)** Scene 98 6/8 Harry in noisy elevator. Heads for top. Conversations bother him.	#1 - HARRY #29 - WOM. IN ELEVATOR #1 #30 - WOM. IN ELEVATOR #2 #31 - MAN IN ELEVATOR <u>EXTRAS</u> Uniformed Gd. Gen Atmos.	#1 EMBARCADERO BLDG. <u>PROPS</u> Blue Pouch Gun/Guard (?) Briefcases for atmos.
	INT. ELEVATOR (D) Scene 199 1/8th Harry in elevator w/ blue pouch - alone.	#1 - HARRY	<u>PROPS</u> Blue Pouch

139

DAY/DATE	SET/SCENES	CAST/ATMOS	STAGE/LOCATION
DAY 13 cont'd	**INT. ELEVATOR (D)** Scenes 276, 277, 280, 281 7/8 Harry gets into elevator. A few stops later, Ann gets on. Harry - nervous. Then they both exit.	# 1 - HARRY # 2 - ANN EXTRAS Atmos - on & off elevator.	PROPS Attache Case
	INT. LOBBY - MR. C'S BLDG. - NEWSSTAND (D) Scenes 366, 367, 368 5/8 Harry looks at paper. Mr. C's on front page.	# 1 - HARRY EXTRAS Gen Atmos Sec. Guard	PROPS Newspapers - Pix of burned M-Benz & Headlines. Blue Pouch

END OF THIRTEENTH DAY

DAY/DATE	SET/SCENES	CAST/ATMOS	STAGE/LOCATION
DAY 14 WEDNESDAY 12/13/--	**INT. MR.C'S SUITE LOBBY & CORRIDOR (D)**	# 1 - HARRY	#1 EMBARCADERO 24TH FLOOR
3-1/8	Scenes 200, 201, 202 203, 204, 205	EXTRAS Janitor	PROPS Trans. Radio Janitorial suppl. Blue Pouch
	1 page		ANIMALS Doberman Pinscher (handler)
	Harry passes janitor spots Doberman. Goes quietly to Mr. C's.		
	INT. MR. C'S SUITE RECEPTION AREA (D)	# 1 - HARRY	PROPS Attache Case Gun f/Guard
	Scenes 273, 274, 275 1-1/8	EXTRAS Receptionist Sec. Guard Atmos.	
	Harry heads for Mr.C's office. Recep. tries to stop him & calls guard. Harry leaves when he sees Mr. C's not there.		

141

DAY/DATE	SET/SCENES	CAST/ATMOS	STAGE/LOCATION
DAY 14 cont'd.	**INT. MR. C'S SUITE RECEPTION AREA (D)** Scenes 369, 370, 371, 372, 373, 374, 375, 376. 1 page Harry & Pouch make it in time to see Ann who sees Harry and indicates to Mark that Harry knows. They leave.	# 1 – HARRY # 2 – ANN # 3 – MARK # 7 – MARTIN EXTRAS Sec. Guard Young Man Atmos. "Crowd"	PROPS Blue Pouch Camera f/press photogs. Guns f/Guards.

END OF FOURTEENTH DAY

DAY/DATE	SET/SCENES	CAST/ATMOS	STAGE/LOCATION
DAY 15 THURSDAY 12/14/--	**INT. SUITE/RECEP/ CORRIDOR/OFFICE (D)**	# 1 - HARRY # 3 - MARK # 7 - MARTIN	#1 EMBARCADERO 41ST FLOOR
3-2/8	Scenes 99, 100, 101, 102. 2-6/8	#20 - MALE RECEPT.	PROPS Blue Pouch PBS & TV Monitors Envelope w/money
	Harry sees recep. who refers him to Martin. Spots Mark. Won't give tape to anyone but Mr. C. he leaves. Sees Mark on way out.	EXTRAS Atmos in off.	

END OF FIFTEENTH DAY

DAY/DATE	SET/SCENES	CAST/ATMOS	STAGE/LOCATION
DAY 16 FRIDAY 12/15/--	**INT. MR. C'S OFF (D)**	# 1 – HARRY # 4 – MR. C # 7 – MARTIN	#1 EMBARCADERO 41ST FLOOR
8-2/8	Scenes 206, 207, 208, 209, 210, 211, 212, 213, 214, 215, 216, 217, 218, 219, 220, 221, 223, 224, 225.		PROPS Blue Pouch w/tapes Recorder Money in Envelope Hearing Aid.
	8-2/8		ANIMALS Doberman Pinscher & Handler

Harry watches dog, sees Mr. C. Fixes hearing aid and turns over tapes. Martin enters and all listen. Tape doesn't incriminate anyone, but Martin is sure there is more. They continue to listen. Mr. C. tells

DAY/DATE	SET/SCENES	CAST/ATMOS	STAGE/LOCATION
DAY 16 cont'd.	Harry that Ann is his wife. Harry is shocked -- asks many un-professional questions. Wants to know what Mr. C. is going to do. Feels responsible. Harry finally leaves. Martin tells him to forget about it.		

END OF SIXTEENTH DAY - END OF THIRD WEEK

DAY/DATE	SET/SCENES	CAST/ATMOS	STAGE/LOCATION
DAY 17 MONDAY	**INT. LAWYER'S OFFICE (D)**	# 1 - HARRY #13 - MCNAUGHT #19 - TONY	PACIFIC STOCK BROKERAGE CO.
12/18/--			
5-2/8	Scenes 93, 94, 95 2-3/8 Harry meets with McNaught and gives him tenants' complaints. They eat during dicussion. Harry and McNaught are friends even if they only speak every once in a while. Harry leaves.		PROPS Blue Pouch Briefcase Slip of paper from tenants. 2 sack lunches. OTHER Teacher?
	Scene 95 2-7/8 Harry & Tony talk about problems. She cries.	# 1 - HARRY #19 - TONY	MAKE-UP Tears

END OF SEVENTEENTH DAY

146

DAY/DATE	SET/SCENES	CAST/ATMOS	STAGE/LOCATION
DAY 18 TUESDAY 12/19/--	**INT. HARRY'S APT.** **BUILDING (D)**	# 1 - HARRY #11 - MRS. GOETNER	700 LAGUNA STREET #306, 307
1-3/8	Scene 40 3/8		PROPS Mailbox key Bills, Ads, Postcard, Laundry Groceries
	Harry collects mail. Mrs. Goetner w/dog says hello, happy birthday. He says hello and goes into his apt.		ANIMALS Dog
	INT. HARRY'S APT (D)	# 1 - HARRY	700 LAGUNA STREET #306, 307
	Scene 41 1 page		PROPS Bottle of wine Mail (incl. post- card) Groceries.
	Harry finds b/day wine, card froms Mrs. Evange- lista. Gets angry at her.		

END OF EIGHTEENTH DAY

147

DAY/DATE	SET/SCENES	CAST/ATMOS	STAGE/LOCATION
DAY 19 WEDNESDAY 12/20/--	**INT. HARRY'S APT. LIV.RM/KITCHEN (N)**	# 1 - HARRY	700 LAGUNA STREET
		#11 - MRS. G.	#306, 307
	Scenes 42,43,44	#12 - RON	
	5-7/8	#13 - MR. CORSITTO	
		#14 - BOB	PROPS
5-7/8		#15 - BOB'S	Wine Bottle
		WIFE	Laundry
	Harry cooks. Hears o/s		Mail
	dialogue. Tries to		Groceries
	eavesdrop w/glass.		Practical sink &
	Almost gets caught by		stove.
	Ron. No hot water.		Pork Chops/cook)
	Other tenants complain.		Tomato & Knife
	Mrs. Goetner brings		Misc. kitch.uten.
	small cake w/4 candles		Plastic madonna
	aflame. Harry is appt'd.		Cupcake w/candles.
	spokesman for tenants.		Broom, glass.
	They leave.		
			CONSTRUCTION
			Pract.trap door
			in closet.

END OF NINETEENTH DAY

148

DAY/DATE	SET/SCENES	CAST/ATMOS	STAGE/LOCATION
DAY 20 THURSDAY 12/21/-- 3-4/8	**EXT. HARRY'S APT. (D)** Scene 49 1/8 Harry exits bldg. Walks to bus stop passing demolition crew.	#1 - HARRY EXTRAS Atmos. Const. Crew	700 LAGUNA STREET MISC Construction Crew & Vehicles (?)
	INT. HARRY'S APT. (N) Scene 48 3/8 Harry plays saxaphone to old recording.	# 1 - HARRY	700 LAGUNA STREET #306, 307 PROPS Stereo set up as designated. Saxaphone (sp?) MISC Jazz rec. to p/b.

149

DAY/DATE	SET/SCENES	CAST/ATMOS	STAGE/LOCATION
DAY 20 cont'd.	**INT. HARRY'S APT.(N)** <u>CORRIDOR</u> Scene 377 4/8 Harry runs to his apt. Passes Ron in hallway.	#1 – HARRY #12 – RON #14 – BOB	700 LAGUNA STREET #306, 307 <u>PROPS</u> Blue Pouch

DAY/DATE	SET/SCENES	CAST/ATMOS	STAGE/LOCATION
DAY 20 cont'd.	**INT. HARRY'S APT.(N)**	# 1 - HARRY	700 LAGUNA STREET
	Scenes 378, 379	#12 - RON (378)	#306, 307
	3 pages	#14 - BOB "	
			PROPS
			Blue Pouch
	Harry goes into apt. Calls Mr. C., not in. They will call him back. Tells them they don't have his #. Neighbors are angry that he is owner. Harry kicks them out of his apt. -- no time to talk now. Phone rings. It is Mark telling Harry that Martin is no longer with firm and Harry should forget all. Mark will be watching.		
	END OF TWENTIETH DAY		

151

DAY/DATE	SET/SCENES	CAST/ATMOS	STAGE/LOCATION
DAY 21 FRIDAY 12/22/-- 3-2/8	**EXT. PHONE BOOTH (D)** Scene 92 1-1/8th Harry calls Mr. C. for appt. to deliver pouch. Gets in and leaves.	# 1 - HARRY EXTRAS Gen St. Atmos	PROPS Blue Pouch Tapes inside. CONST. Telephone Booth Neon Sign
COMPANY MOVES TO 765 MISSION STREET			

152

DAY/DATE	SET/SCENES	CAST/ATMOS	STAGE/LOCATION
DAY 21 cont'd.	**INT. CATHOLIC CHURCH CONFESSIONAL (D)**	# 1 – HARRY	765 MISSION ST.
	Scenes 230, 231 6/8	EXTRAS Priest (o/s) Boy (14 yrs) Atmos-church	PROPS Blue Pouch
	Scene 230 (2/8) – Harry goes into church.		NOTES Welfare Worker?
	Scene 231 (4/8) – Goes to confessional, tells all, but...		
	INT. LAUNDRY (D)	# 1 – HARRY #27 – L/LADY #28 – L/L BOY	PROPS Harry's Laundry Money
	Scene 39 5/8	EXTRAS Atmos.	Groceries Glass/water Dish towel
	Harry does trick, gets laundry & goes.		NOTES Welfare worker

153

DAY/DATE	SET/SCENES	CAST/ATMOS	STAGE/LOCATION
DAY 21 cont'd.	**INT. AUD/SLIDES**		PROPS Blue box, car(nd) Diagrams
	Scenes 120 (part), 123, 125	EXTRAS Woman/blue box	NOTES Slides which will be used later in Convention Scene
	Scene 120 (3/8) – Car speeding through city.		
	Scene 123 (2/8) – CU of blue box, and diagram of interference.		
	Scene 125 (1/8) – Pretty woman installs blue box.		
END OF TWENTY-FIRST DAY – END OF FOURTH WEEK.			
* * * * * CHRISTMAS & NEW YEAR'S BREAK * * * * *			

154

Shooting Schedule

DAY/DATE	SET/SCENES	CAST/ATMOS	STAGE/LOCATION
DAY 22 WEDNESDAY 1/3/--	**EXT. CONTINENTAL LODGE (D)**	# 1 - HARRY	2550 VAN NESS CONTINENTAL VAGABOND MOTEL
1-3/8	Scenes 232, 233, 234 235, 236	EXTRAS Gen. Atmos.	PROPS Attache case.
5/8	Harry goes to motel looks it over, and registers.		
	INT. CONTINENTAL LOBBY (D)	# 1 - HARRY #36 - CLERK	2550 VAN NESS
	Scene 237 3/8		PROPS Attache case Motel Key Registration
	Harry wants room B-7 but settles for room next door.		

155

DAY/DATE	SET/SCENES	CAST/ATMOS	STAGE/LOCATION
DAY 22 cont'd.	**INT. CONTINENTAL CORRIDOR (D)** Scene 238 2/8 Harry goes to his room. Room B-7 is definitely occupied.	#1 – HARRY	PROPS Attache case "Do not disturb" sign – B-7 Room key.
	INT. CONTINENTAL CORRIDOR (N) Scene 254 1/8th Do Not Disturb sign is gone. Harry picks lock and goes in B-7.	#1 – HARRY	PROPS Ring of lock picks

END OF TWENTY-SECOND DAY

DAY/DATE	SET/SCENES	CAST/ATMOS	STAGE/LOCATION
DAY 23 THURSDAY 1/4/--	**INT. MOTEL, ROOM B-5** **HARRY'S - (D)**	# 1 - HARRY	2550 VAN NESS CONTINENTAL LODGE
2-6/8	Scenes 239, 240, 241, 242, 243, 244, 245, 246, 247, 248, 249, 250.		PROPS Attache Case Motel Key Jeweller's Drill "Bug" Elect. Box
	2-3/8		CONSTRUCTION Putty & Matching touch-up paint in case Take 1 isn't a Print.
	Harry goes into room. Goes to window. POV B-7 with curtains drawn. Goes back. Puts bug under sink and hears violent sounds coming from B-7. Stops listening, turns on tv full blast. Hides in bed.		

157

DAY/DATE	SET/SCENES	CAST/ATMOS	STAGE/LOCATION
DAY 23 cont'd.	**INT. MOTEL ROOM B-5 HARRY'S - (N)** Scenes 251, 252, 253. 3/8 Harry wakes up. Quiet next door. His TV still blaring. Harry goes to Room B-7 to look.	# 1 - HARRY	<u>PROPS</u> Attache Case Motel Key

END OF TWENTY-THIRD DAY

DAY/DATE	SET/SCENES	CAST/ATMOS	STAGE/LOCATION
DAY 24 FRIDAY 1/5/--	**INT. MOTEL ROOM B-7 (N)**	# 1 - HARRY	2550 VAN NESS CONTINENTAL LODGE (INCL. PREVIOUS FOOTAGE)
2-3/8ths	Scenes 255, 256, 257, 258, 259, 260.		
	6/8ths		PROPS
	Room is straight. No "body" in sight. Harry checks all, goes into bathroom.		Lock Picks Motel Ads Sanitized glasses

DAY/DATE	SET/SCENES	CAST/ATMOS	STAGE/LOCATION
DAY 24 cont'd.	**INT. BATHROOM B-7 (N)**	#1 - HARRY	EFX Water in toilet becomes bloody.
	Scenes 261, 262, 263, 264, 265, 266, 267, 268, 270, 270.		
	1-3/8ths		
	Bathroom is ok, but toilet won't stop running. Harry tries to stop it -- fills up with blood. And over flows. Harry is scared to death. He runs out of bathroom to get air.		

DAY/DATE	SET/SCENES	CAST/ATMOS	STAGE/LOCATION
DAY 24 cont'd.	**INT. MOTEL ROOM & BATHROOM (repeat) (N)**	# 1 - HARRY	
	Scene 354 1/8th		
	Harry tracks blood on tile and carpet.		
	EXT. MOTEL WINDOW B-7) (N)	#1 - HARRY	
	Scene 269 1/8th		
	POV Harry getting air at window.		

END OF TWENTY-FOURTH DAY - END OF FIFTH WEEK

DAY/DATE	SET/SCENES	CAST/ATMOS	STAGE/LOCATION
DAY 25 MONDAY 1/8/--	**INT. B-7 MOTEL ROOM & BATH (D)**	#2 - ANN	2550 VAN NESS CONTINENTAL LODGE
1-3/8	Scenes 363, 359, 360, 361, 356	#3 - MARK	
	1-3/8	#4 - MR. C.	PROPS
			Plastic Sheet
	Scene 363 (2/8) - Mr. C. plays tape for Ann and Mark. Mark locks door.		Bloody Tissues Short-bladed knives Blood
	Scenes 359, 360, 361. (6/8) - Mr. C is killed with small knives.		EFX Stab wounds on body. Blood.
	Scene 356 (3/8) - Bloody tissue in toilet. Mark cleans off walls. Mr. C on plastic sheet to catch drips.		

END OF TWENTY-FIFTH DAY

DAY/DATE	SET/SCENES	CAST/ATMOS	STAGE/LOCATION
DAYS 26&27 TUESDAY 1/9/-- WEDNESDAY 1/10/-- 5-4/8	**EXT/INT. BUS #1(D)** Scenes 284, 285, 289, 291. 4/8	# 2 - ANN #37 - DRIVER BUS #1 #38-DRIVER #2	CLAY ST., 6TH STREET FULTON
	Sc. 284 - Bus in fog (1/8)	EXTRAS Passengers	EFX Fog?
	Sc. 285 - Moving on Ann in bus. (1/8)		
	Sc. 289 - Ext. Moving view on bus (on hill) (1/8).		
	Sc. 291 - Moving View on Ann's bus. (1/8).		

163

DAY/DATE	SET/SCENES	CAST/ATMOS	STAGE/LOCATION
	INT. BUS #1 (D)	#1 – HARRY #2 – ANN #38 – DRIVER BUS #2	
	Scenes 298, 300, 301, 302. 1-3/8		PROPS Attache Case
		EXTRAS Passengers	
	Sc. 298 (3/8) Harry gets on behind Ann.		
	Scs. 300, 301, 302 (1 pg.) Harry talks to Ann. She moves away. He follows.		
	EXT. BUS #1 (LATE AFTERNOON (D)	#1 – HARRY #2 – ANN #38 – DRIVER #2	PROPS Attache Case
	Scene 299 (1/8) Bus through thickening fog.	EXTRAS Passengers	

DAY/DATE	SET/SCENES	CAST/ATMOS	STAGE/LOCATION
DAYS 26&27 cont'd.	**EXT. BUS #1 (N)**	#1 – HARRY	
		#2 – ANN	
	Scs. 303, 304.	#37 – DRIVER #1	PROPS
	2/8		Attache Case
		EXTRAS	
	Bus through night.	Passengers	
	Ann tries to ignore		
	Harry who's behind her.		
	INT. BUS #1 (N)	# 1 – HARRY	CLAY STREET
		# 2 – ANN	6TH STREET
	Scenes 305, 306	#37 – DRIVER	FULTON
	1-6/8	BUS #1	
		EXTRAS	PROPS
	Harry talks to Ann	Atmos on bus.	Attache case
	who isn't interested.		
	He repeats part of the		
	"Ann/Mark" tape -- she's		
	scared and runs. He		
	follows her.		

165

DAY/DATE	SET/SCENES	CAST/ATMOS	STAGE/LOCATION
DAYS 26&27 cont'd.	**EXT. POLES & LINES (INSERTS)** (D)		CLAY ST. SIXTH ST. FULTON ST.
	Scenes 286, 290, 294. 3/8.		
	Scene 286 (1/8) Wires short.		
	Scene 290 (1/8) Wires separate.		
	Scene 294 (1/8) Antennae glide straight		
	EXT. STREET & HARRY'S BUS (D)	#1 – HARRY #39 – DRIVER #2	PROPS Attache Case
	Sc. 297 1/8	EXTRAS Passengers	
	Harry gets off, falls down, goes to Ann's bus. Gets on.	STUNT DOUBLE?	

END OF TWENTY-SIXTH AND TWENTY-SEVENTH DAYS.

DAY/DATE	SET/SCENES	CAST/ATMOS	STAGE/LOCATION
DAYS 26&27 cont'd.	**INT. BUS #2 & STREET** (D)	#1 - HARRY #38-DRIVER #2	<u>PROPS</u>
	Scenes 287, 288, 292, 293, 295, 296.	<u>EXTRAS</u> Passengers	
	7/8		
	Sc. 287. (1/8) Moving view on Harry.		
	Sc. 288 (1/8) POV Bus #1		
	Sc. 292 (1/8) Bus #2 climbs hill.		
	Sc. 293 (1/8) Harry watches Ann's bus.		
	Sc. 295 (1/8) Moving view - Bus #2.		
	Sc. 296 (2/8) Harry gets up, heads for Ann's bus.		

167

DAY/DATE	SET/SCENES	CAST/ATMOS	STAGE/LOCATION
DAYS 26&27 cont'd.	EXT. BUS & STREET (N)	#1 – HARRY #2 – ANN	
	Scenes 307, 308 3/8	#38 – DRIVER BUS #2	PROPS Attache Case
			EFX Fog?
	Ann runs onto stairs. Harry follows, trying to make her listen.		

168

DAY/DATE	SET/SCENES	CAST/ATMOS	STAGE/LOCATION
DAY 28 THURSDAY 1/11/--	**EXT. STEPPED ST. (N)**	# 1 - HARRY	PROPS
	Scenes 309, 310, 311, 312, 313, 314, 315, 316.	# 2 - ANN	Attache Case
5-4/8			EFX
	1-1/8		Fog
	Harry says he's a good person. Ann runs.		

DAY/DATE	SET/SCENES	CAST/ATMOS	STAGE/LOCATION
	EXT. PARK (N)	# 1 - HARRY	PROPS
		# 2 - ANN	Attache Case
	Scenes 317, 318, 319,		
	321, 322, 323,		EFX
	324, 325, 326,		
	327, 328, 329,		
	330, 331, 332.		
	4-3/8		
	Harry follows Ann into park & tells all. When he's done, she's gone.		

END OF TWENTY-EIGHTH DAY

DAY/DATE	SET/SCENES	CAST/ATMOS	STAGE/LOCATION
DAY 29 FRIDAY 1/12/--	**INT. HARRY'S RM (D)**	#1 - HARRY	700 LAGUNA ST.

2-7/8ths	Scs. 380, 381, 382, 383, 384, 385, 386, 387, 388, 389, 390, 391, 392, 393, 394, 395, 396, 367/		PROPS
			Saxophone
			Records
			Pencil Screw-
			  driver
			Telephone,
			Wall Switches
			to take apart.
			Knife to slit
			  sofa.
			Bowl of hot
			  water.
			Razor blade.
			Screwdriver.
			Sponge.

Harry plays sax. Phone rings. No one there. Becomes paranoid. Takes phone apart-- nothing. Takes plates from wall, moves chairs, rolls up carpet, checks Madonna-- still nothing. Checks walls for wires, peels paper, rips up baseboard, floorboards, Again...nothing.

END OF TWENTY-NINTH DAY

171

DAY/DATE	SET/SCENES	CAST/ATMOS	STAGE/LOCATION
DAYS 30&31 MONDAY 1/15/--	**EXT. HARRY'S WAREHOUSE (D)**	#1 - HARRY	255 KANSAS ST.
	Scene 50 2/8	EXTRAS Warehouse Types	PROPS Asst'd. Boxes
	Harry enters elev.		EFX Practical elev.
TUESDAY 1/16/-- 11-6/8	**INT. WAREHOUSE (D)**	#1 - HARRY #5 - STAN	PROPS Tape Tape Recorders Magazines Coffee & Pot Filter Device (Sc. 80) Photo - Ann/Mark.
	Scenes 51, 52, 53, 54, 55, 56, 57, 59, 60, 61, 63, 65, 67, 69, 70, 72, 73, 74, 75, 76, 77, 78, 79, 80, 82, 83, 84, 85, 86, 88, 89, 90, 91.		

172

DAY/DATE	SET/SCENES	CAST/ATMOS	STAGE/LOCATION
DAYS 30&31 cont'd.	**INT. WAREHOUSE (D) — cont'd.**		
	Scs. 51, 52, 53, 54 55, 56, 57. 2-6/8 — Harry and Stan work on tapes. Tells Harry about convention. Gets coffee.		
	Scs. 59, 60, 61.(3/8) Harry works.		
	Sc. 63. (4/8) — Harry listens.		
	Scs. 65, 67. (3-4/8) Harry listens. Stan is a pest. Harry yells at him -- Stanley leaves.		

173

DAY/DATE	SET/SCENES	CAST/ATMOS	STAGE/LOCATION
DAYS 30&31 cont'd.	**INT. WAREHOUSE (D) – cont'd.** Scs. 69, 70. (4/8) Harry listens to tapes. Scs. 72, 73, 74, 75, 76, 77, 78, 79, 80. (1-3/8) Harry listens. Adds a special filter. Scs. 82, 83, 84, 85, 86. (1 page) – Harry hears "kill us" and is upset. Scs. 88, 89, 90, 91. (4/8) Harry rewinds tape, looks at photo of Ann & Mark.		

END OF THIRTIETH AND THIRTY-FIRST DAYS

174

DAY/DATE	SET/SCENES	CAST/ATMOS	STAGE/LOCATION
DAYS 32, 33, 34	**INT. WAREHOUSE (N)**	#1 - HARRY #5 - STAN #6 - PAUL #8 - MORAN #9 - MEREDITH #10 - MILLARD #17 - LURLEEN	255 KANSAS ST.
WEDNESDAY 1/17/--	Scs. 160, 161, 162, 163, 164, 165, 166, 167, 168, 169, 170, 171, 172, 173.		PROPS 4 bottles whisky ice sack beer cans bag potato chips cups f/drinks record player records
THURSDAY 1/18/--	19-4/8		Mark/Ann tape (to (play)
FRIDAY 1/19/--	All arrive, have party. Harry & Meredith dance.		Name tags
19-4/8	Paul cuts in. Moran tells about welfare fund. Harry tells him about bugged bait		O/N bag Pen (Moran's ad)

continued....

175

DAY/DATE	SET/SCENES	CAST/ATMOS	STAGE/LOCATION
DAYS 32, 33, 34	**INT. WAREHOUSE (N) – cont'd.** tank. Mark/Ann tape plays. Harry upset. Harry talks about current surveillance problem. Won't let Moran see any of his stuff. Moran plays back "Harry/Meredith" tape. Embarrassed and upset he kicks them all out. Meredith stays.		Bookshelf w/radios, ashtrays, packs of cigarettes, cigar humidors, vases, etc. Bouquet w/mike Cig. pack – elect. components Blackboard/chalk Cassette recorder (Moran) Cot & Blanket <u>EFX</u> Light change

END OF THIRTY-SECOND, THIRTY-THIRD AND THIRTY-FOURTH DAYS

END OF SEVENTH WEEK

176

DAY/DATE	SET/SCENES	CAST/ATMOS	STAGE/LOCATION
DAYS 35&36	**INT. WAREHOUSE (N)**	# 1 - HARRY # 9 -MEREDITH	255 KANSAS ST.
MONDAY 1/22/--	Scs. 174, 175, 176, 177, 178, 179 180, 181, 183, 184.		PROPS 4 bottles whisky ice sack beer cans bag potato chips cups f/drinks record player records
TUESDAY 1/23/--			Mark/Ann tape (to play) Name tags O/N bag Pen (Moran's ad)
10-1/8			Bookshelf w/radios, ashtrays, packs
10-6/8	Meredith and Harry talk about his work. He replays Ann/Mark tape. Harry listens. Meredith undresses, then undresses Harry. He is not interested. Meredith persists. He gives in. They fall asleep on sofa. Harry dreams and sleeps .		of cigarettes, cigar humidors, vases, etc. Bouquet w/mike

DAY/DATE	SET/SCENES	CAST/ATMOS	STAGE/LOCATION
DAYS 35&36 cont'd.	**INT. WAREHOUSE (N) - cont'd.**		PROPS - cont'd. Cig. pack - elect. components Blackboard/chalk Cassette recorder (Moran) Cot & Blanket EFX Light change
	INT. WAREHOUSE (N) #1 - HARRY Scs. 186, 187. 5/8 Harry wakes up. Meredith gone, phone humming.		PROPS Phone Cot & Blanket

END OF THIRTY-FIFTH AND THIRTY-SIXTH DAYS

178

DAY/DATE	SET/SCENES	CAST/ATMOS	STAGE/LOCATION
DAY 37	**INT. WAREHOUSE (N)**	#1 - HARRY	255 KANSAS STREET
WEDNESDAY 1/24/-- 5-1/8	Scenes 337, 338, 339, 340, 341, 342, 343, 344, 345, 346, 347, 348, 349, 350, 351, 352, 353, 355, 357, 358, 362, 364.		PROPS Attache Case Beer Can EFX Light Change (Off/On)

4-6/8

Scs. 337 thru 353 - Harry creeps upstairs. Kicks beer can, is startled. Lights go out. He continues. Turns lights back on. Hears Mark/Ann tape playing. Sees everything has been searched. Goes to window. Sees two men running away. Plays tapes again -- discovers new information. (3-6/8)

DAY/DATE	SET/SCENES	CAST/ATMOS	STAGE/LOCATION
DAY 37 cont'd.	**INT. WAREHOUSE (N) – cont'd.**		
	Sc. 355 – Harry remembers bloody shoes. (2/8)		
	Scs. 357, 358 – Harry listens to tape (3/8)		
	Sc. 362 – Harry sees it all (1/8)		
	Sc. 364 – Shuts off recorder. (1/8).		

DAY/DATE	SET/SCENES	CAST/ATMOS	STAGE/LOCATION
DAY 37 cont'd.	**EXT. WAREHOUSE ALLEY (N)**	#1 – HARRY	<u>PROPS</u> Attache Case
	Scenes 333, 334, 335, 336.		
	4/8		
	Harry sees lights on in warehouse. Goes to see what is going. Uses stairs -- not elevator.		

END OF THIRTY-SEVENTH DAY

DAY/DATE	SET/SCENES	CAST/ATMOS	STAGE/LOCATION
DAY 38	**INT. CAR (TRAVELING)** **(N)**	# 1-HARRY # 5-STAN	PROPS Sedan (Paul)
THURSDAY 1/25/--	Scenes 144, 146, 147, 148, 149, 151, 152, 153, 155, 157, 158, 159.	# 6-PAUL # 8-MORAN # 9-MEREDITH #10-MILLARD #17-LURLEEN	Mustang (Willie) License as desc. or as/is. Radio in sedan
3 pages	2-4/8	#35-WILLIE/YNG STUNT.DBL FOR WILLIE	DRIVER VEHICLES Staff Car (Sedan) Mustang
	Sc. 144 - Introductions as Mustang passes Paul. Paul tails them. (4/8)		
	Sc. 146 - Paul pulls up next to Mustang (2/8)		
	Scs. 147, 148 - Field car? (2/8)		

continued...

DAY/DATE	SET/SCENES	CAST/ATMOS	STAGE/LOCATION
DAY 38	**INT. CAR (TRAVELING) – cont'd. (N)**		
	Sc. 149 – Lurlee wants them to stop. Paul #1 Tail Man and can't. (3/8).		
	Scs. 151, 152, 153, 155 – Stan says Paul is "Bullitt". Paul checks out license plate. (6/8)		
	Scs. 157, 158. Meredith is bugged. Paul calls Mustang driver by name, "WILLIE" (2/8)		
	Sc. 159 – Staff car pulls away from Willie who is amazed. (1/8)		

DAY/DATE	SET/SCENES	CAST/ATMOS	STAGE/LOCATION	PROPS
DAY 38 cont'd.	**EXT. STREET – SEDAN AND MUSTANG (N)**	# 1–HARRY		PROPS
	Scenes 145, 150, 154, 156.	# 5–STAN		
		# 6–PAUL		
		# 8–MORAN		
		# 9–MEREDITH		
		#10–MILLARD		
	4/8	#17–LURLEEN		
		#35–WILLIE/YNG DRIVER		
		STUNT DOUBLE/WILLIE		
	Sc. 145 – Paul chases Mustang (1/8)			
	Sc. 150 – Mustang careens around corner – almost out of control. (1/8)			
	Sc. 154 – CU – Mustang's license plates. (1/8)			
	Sc. 156 – Paul pulls up next to Mustang at light. (1/8)			

END OF THIRTY-EIGHTH DAY

184

DAY/DATE	SET/SCENES	CAST/ATMOS	STAGE/LOCATION
DAY 39	**INT. CONVENTION BAR (N)**	# 1 – HARRY #7 – MARTIN	ST. FRANCIS HOTEL GRAND BALLROOM
FRIDAY 1/26/--	Scenes 133 – 136. 1-5/8		PROPS Pay Phone Liquor for people at bar. Draft beer for Martin.
6-6/8	Harry makes phone call. Disconnected number. Accosted by Mr. C's assistant (Martin). Told to bring pouch on Sunday. Martin asks what's on tapes. Harry ignores him, and goes back to convention.		

185

DAY/DATE	SET/SCENES	CAST/ATMOS	STAGE/LOCATION
DAY 39 cont'd.	**INT. CONVENTION BOOTH AREA (N)**	# 1-HARRY # 6-PAUL # 5-STAN # 9-MEREDITH # 7-MARTIN #10-MILLARD #17-LURLEEN # 8 MORAN IN B/R #43 1ST WOMAN IN B/R	PROPS Walkie-Talkie Loudspeaker O/Night case- Meredith.
	Scenes 137, 138, 139, 140, 141, 142. 4-3/8 Paul grabs Harry. Takes him to Moran. They've bugged the Ladies' Room. They listen. Stan on guard at door with walkie-talkie. Woman exits. Then Meredith. They're joined by Bill and Lurleen. They leave for Harry's warehouse.	EXTRAS 125 mixed business types men & women.	

DAY/DATE	SET/SCENES	CAST/ATMOS	STAGE/LOCATION
DAY 39 cont'd.	**EXT. PARKING LOT (N)**	# 1-HARRY	PROPS
		# 5-STAN	Grey sedan w/
	Scene 143. (6/8)	# 6-PAUL	official seal.
		# 8-MORAN	
		#10-MILLARD	
	They all get into	#17-LURLEEN	
	Paul's car and leave.	# 9-MEREDITH	
		EXTRAS	
		Pkg Attdnt.	
		Atmos as needed.	

END OF THIRTY-NINTH DAY

END OF EIGHTH WEEK

DAY/DATE	SET/SCENES	CAST/ATMOS	STAGE/LOCATION
DAY 40	**INT. CONVENTION** <u>**LOBBY/BOOTH AREA**</u>	#1-HARRY #34-MAN/BOOTH #7-MARTIN	ST. FRANCIS HOTEL GRAND BALLROOM
MONDAY 1/29/--			
4 pages	Scenes 109, 110, 111, 112, 113, 114, 115, 116, 117, 119.	<u>EXTRAS</u> Hostesses Conventioneers	<u>PROPS</u> White name cards. Components "L-T 500. Drinks. Name card -- "HARRY CAUL"
	2-3/8		
	Harry goes into convention. Gets name tag. Views display, moves toward auditorium.		
	Scene 118 (1/8) - Harry's POV of Martin in crowd.		

DAY/DATE	SET/SCENES	CAST/ATMOS	STAGE/LOCATION
DAY 40 cont'd.	**INT. CONVENTION AUDITORIUM (N)**	# 1-HARRY # 6-PAUL #33-SPEAKER	PROPS Name Cards Paper/Speaker Slides as desc. Flyers is bags.
	Scenes 120(part),121, 122, 123, 124.	EXTRAS Audience	
	1-5/8		
	Harry goes into slide show. Paul spots him. Takes him off for a drink.		NOTE - page Credit for 121 taken on Day 21.

END OF FORTIETH DAY

DAY/DATE	SET/SCENES	CAST/ATMOS	STAGE/LOCATION
DAY 41	**INT. CONVENTION** **BOOTH AREA (N)**	# 1-HARRY # 6-PAUL # 5-STAN # 8-MORAN # 9-MEREDITH #45 MAN IN # BOOTH #2	ST. FRANCIS HOTEL (MAIN BALLROOM) PROPS Name tags Fly sheets Pillow Cigarettes Drinks Red Telephone Moran S-15 bug Harmonica Sign: "BOOTH 34 WILLIAM P. MORAN & ASSOCIATES."
TUESDAY 1/30/-- 8-7/8	Scenes 126, 127, 128. 8-7/8 Harry and Paul go to Moran's booth and see S-15 demo. Dialogue w/Stan. He goes. Harry talks w/bystander and demo man. Harry won't endorse product. He leaves.		

END OF FORTY-FIRST DAY

END OF NINTH WEEK...END OF SHOW!!

X
FINAL COMMENTS

After many days of hard work, your production board is now fully laid out. You have calculated that it will take 41 days to shoot the scripted material, including two weeks of Second Camera work which was scheduled to be done with the First Camera work. This gives you the opportunity to have greater coverage of the material which is scheduled for the first two working weeks.

You have now gone through THE CONVERSATION. You have broken down and scheduled one of the more complicated scripts and will be ready now to learn how to turn all this information into a budget. That is covered fully in *Film Budgeting.*

Here are a few more hints which might help you on your next (or first) feature project.

1) After finishing your breakdown, go over each day's schedule with the director and see if he agrees with it. It is important that the director be enthusiastic about your schedule and believe that he can shoot it. He should understand it and believe that it is realistically laid out. Going over the board very carefully with the director will

give you the opportunity to understand how he thinks. The more you understand the way the director thinks, the more accurately you will be able to lay out your schedule. Remember, you are scheduling the show in the best way the director can shoot it—not the best way that *you* would shoot it.

2) Understand that a director may want to add a scene or expand a scene (or drop scenes). As the creative force on the picture, he has that privilege and you must be flexible enough to be able to deal with it. Your schedule must be able to be re-arranged or altered if and when the need arises. If you feel that the suggested change will add more than reasonable costs to the picture, then you should make the director and the producer aware in a diplomatic way.

3) The question, "what if . . .?" will haunt you every day on a production. A production manager's role is flexible. He must constantly be building alternate routes for each and every day. As a type of Line Quarterback for the producer and/or studio, it is his responsibility to keep the film moving along on a straight course.

If a film company stops shooting or is delayed in any way, the flow of dollars does not necessarily stop. If the production is not gaining ground each day towards completing pages of the script, then massive losses are as certain as getting your feet wet from the massive tidal wave you are watching.

4) Communication is so essential that it cannot be over-stressed. A production manager is middle management—the link between the production and those who are responsible for the total costs of the project. If the production manager maintains a solid and open communication sys-

tem with both sides, he will be far ahead of the game in problem-solving and, therefore, on the way to a more smoothly run production.

5) Keep organized. One way we have found is to keep your breakdown sheets with you at all times. They were your first contact with the script and, quite possibly, will be your most complete notes. Before you start shooting, we have found that it is a good idea to re-arrange them into the order of the production schedule, marking them with dividers. If your copy machine reduces, then you can reduce everything. It makes it much easier to carry it around. Include a map to the location for every scene and list the people to contact about that location. Also include a separate section with your cast and crew list, contact sheet, location list, etc. A good supply of note paper inserted into your book will be invaluable. Tape two or three pens inside the cover, and make sure you have a good supply of dimes for calling the production office. Rarely do locations have telephones which you may use. Most likely, you will find yourself on a street corner using the local public telephone. This book will be your production Bible—your ready reference to any question which may come up. Keep it up-to-date. If a scene changes, do a new breakdown sheet and put it in its proper place.

As you do more script breakdowns, you will find that the work goes more quickly. Playing the various roles of producer, director, actor, stunt coordinator, special effects coordinator, etc., can be a lot of fun.

GOOD LUCK! I'd love to hear from you and of your successes in production.

Let's make movies!!!

XI

FILM SCHEDULING
&
THE COMPUTER

Since *FILM SCHEDULING* was originally published in 1984, many things have changed in our lives. Companies are considered out of date if they don't have fax machines... executives not only have car phones, but also call-waiting and answering machines on those car phones. Some even have fax machines in their cars! The personal computer is now a standard piece of office equipment. And the portable computer is fast gaining acceptance as a replacement for the briefcase.

It is not uncommon to see computers—Mac's and PC's, portable and desktop models—being used every day in motion picture and television production. Production coordinators use them to keep track of all the paperwork which a film company generates. How much simpler it is to make changes in the Cast & Crew List on a computer rather than the old-fashioned way of whiting out and/or cutting and pasting...or even re-typing! And the production accounting function has been computerized for years. Now instead of having to wait five days for a cost report to see where we stand, we can have them instantly!

Computers have also made their way into the scheduling process for filmmaking. What a godsend, you say. And, in many respects, you are right. The constant re-arranging of strips on the production board is, probably, one of the most tedious jobs a production manager or assistant director has to do, except, perhaps, lining the script or filling in the breakdown sheets. Wouldn't it be great if there were a computer program that would do all that for you? Or how about a program that would break down the entire script and do a schedule at the same time the script was being typed into the computer?

Before you go rushing to your nearest computer store to buy this miracle program, let me offer some words of advice and caution. The most effective production manager must know his project better than anyone else on the show—including the director. The only way I am able to get to know a project that well is to work on it, and work on it, and work on it. When you are on location in the middle of a very expensive night shoot and a question needs to be answered immediately, you don't have time to search your notes or your records...or even consult your computer. You are expected to have the answers at your fingertips. What cover set can we use if it rains today? Which actors are working tomorrow and how will it affect their turn-around time if we go over schedule tonight? Etc., etc.

The best program is only as good as its user. The old theory of garbage in-garbage out is especially true when it comes to computers and scheduling a film project. Let me digress a little and tell you a true story. In 1981, I saw a demonstration of a computer program for scheduling a film developed by two people—one a computer expert, and one a seasoned production manager. It sounded like heaven. It was so sophisticated that it really could take a script typed in by a typist and produce a complete production schedule without any additional input from the production manager. It could also prepare full lists of sets, props, animals, special effects, cast, etc., a Day-Out-Of-Days and call sheets, if necessary. What an amazing program! When I saw it, the only bug it had was that the computer was having a hard time with the term "baseball bat." It put "baseball" under Props, and "bat" under Animals with the notation that we needed a "bat wrangler" Once the minor adjustment was made, the program would be perfect. Anyone could create a schedule! The problem was that no one knew that schedule, much less the show. And the creators knew this. They decided to make their program less sophisticated so that the purchasers would be less inclined to let the computer do all the work. To my knowledge, this program never was released.

Now a decade later, there are other programs on the market which basically do the same thing. We have smaller computers which are faster and more powerful than their early cousins from the 1980s. Use them to your advantage, but do not expect them to do your work for you. Read your script again and again. Line your script and then type the information into the breakdown page of the computer program. (As breakdown pages are usually used to arrange and sort the information so that the production secretary can type a shooting schedule, they are not really needed any more. If needed, most programs will print out breakdown pages.) Most production managers who use computers find it is impossible to completely schedule a show on the computer screen—there is just not enough information displayed for the whole show. A suggestion from fellow production manager and Directors Guild of America member Walt Gilmore (see information below), is to rough sort the strips by "auto-sort," by location or studio, exterior or interior, set or scene number. Then print out the strips and mount them on the board in that order. After studying the strips, manually move the strips into rough days and weeks, adjusting for availability of sets and cast. From this point on, it is simpler to sort the strips on the computer as you can see one full week at a time on the screen, making it easier to adjust the individual days. When you are happy with the schedule, save it to disk and then try to improve it. When several versions have been saved, print them out and compare them. When your schedule is set, then have your program print out the shooting schedule, Day-Out-Of-Days Cast List, Set Lists, etc.

Check, double-check and re-check is the name of the game. The computer is excellent for making changes. For example, changing a name on a Cast List corrects all the reports: changing the name of a set changes it everywhere. Page counts changed on a strip then change the day total and picture total.

Most of what the computer can do is fairly mind-boggling and should help you in your job. But do not rely on your computer program to save you from making mistakes. Remember a few words of caution... "To err is human, but to really foul things up takes a computer." And, of course, always back-up your work...everyday.

Each program has its benefits and limitations. The best way to find out about a program is to get the demonstration disk, if available, or arrange for a personal, or group, demonstration. Read the different companies' pamphlets, see several demonstrations and then take a second, private, demonstration of at least two programs where you can spend some time at the computer inputting 15-20 breakdown pages and creating a sample schedule. Also get feedback from other people using the program. Obviously your choices will be mitigated by which computer you choose to use—Mac or PC. We use Macs in our office as they are a "kinder, gentler" computer for those of us who are not "computer friendly." The choice is yours. Remember, that a computer is a tool, just like a fax machine or car phone. It should be used to help solve your problems, not create new ones.

The following advice and list of computer programs currently available together with the Shopper's Checklist were compiled by Walt Gilmore, Chairman of the Computer Committee of the Directors Guild of America.

"Computers really allow a schedule to be typed by a

$2000 a week Assistant Director instead of a $400 a week secretary! This is all right if the use of a computer lets the Assistant Director spend more time understanding the script, planning the production and managing the set. The computer should reduce the time spent doing paper work and make for better planning and more accurate reports and schedules. In addition, the computer should allow for more accurate assessment of production options and the creation of better records.

"The following is a list of available production programs. These programs cover a wide range of variable features and Hardware requirements Some of the programs work in a text mode, reducing the Ram and drive (or disk storage) capacity. Other programs operate in a graphics mode, requiring a graphics board and allowing more sophisticated displays (i.e., the Macintosh mouse-icon display) on the monitor. There are many other variables between the programs which, on the surface, may be of less concern to the user (size of files, speed of printing, etc.) but may affect the user when working on very large, complicated projects. The *user-interface* (how the user operates the program) is probably of more concern to most people. If you are uncomfortable with the changes that you must make in your working environment to use the program, it will not satisfy you. That is why the buyer must be familiar with what is available and try at least two before purchasing.

"The descriptions below are by no means complete— merely attempts to reflect the major features and differences of each program. I have attempted to standardize the terminology used in the individual companies' brochures and reduce the information to the essentials. In this editing, my personal preferences are naturally included. Therefore, when shopping, please use this list as a guide to your own investigation. A check list to use as a guide to shopping follows.

"Except as noted, all programs have some sort of security system on the master disk to stop usable copies from being made. A limited number of usable copies can be installed on hard disks."

—Walt Gilmore

PRODUCTION SOFTWARE SUMMARY
Compiled by Walt Gilmore
Computer Committee Chairperson
Directors Guild of America

AD/80
Alnitak Computing
1326 Greenwich Street
San Francisco, CA   94109
Tel. 415/771-8008
Compuserve 74035,663

Minimum system requirements:
Macintosh: Not Available
MS-DOS: 64K RAM , 2-Double Sided, Double Density Floppy Drives. Mouse and graphics adaptor not required.

Program description: Newly updated and streamlined program for scheduling. A text mode program that compactly does the basic scheduling job with no frills. The program includes a file of blank forms on a disk. The program will work on any MS-DOS computer with two disk drives. No security is used on this program. Created by a DGA assistant director. Available to DGA members through the DGA. Also available through Compuserve.

Price: Shareware - Suggested $100 donation.

DOTZERO, INC.
702 Third Street
Hermosa Beach, California 90254
Tel. 213/376-7732
FAX 213/379-5103

Minimum system requirements:
Macintosh: Not Available
MS-DOS: 256K RAM, 10 MB Hard Disk or 2-Double Sided High Density floppy drives. Mouse and graphics adaptor not required.

Program Description: A brand new version of the original production schedule program. Sold on a stand-alone basis, with additional fees for technical advice. Designed to be so simple that all questions are answered by pushing the F1 Help Key. A budgeting program is in development.

Price: $200. A demo disk which allows you to try a limited version of the program for ten days is available for $25.

THE FILM PRODUCTION TOOLKIT
c/o Mr. Don Asquith
3114 Fifth Street
Santa Monica, CA 90405
Tel. 213/396-1199

Minimum System Requirements:
Macintosh: See MAC TOOLKIT below.
MS-DOS: 256K RAM, 10 MB Hard Disk or 1-Double Sided High Density floppy drive and 1-Double Sided Double Density floppy drive. Mouse and graphics adaptor required.

Program Description: Each program uses a security key module which plugs into the parallel port. This program introduced Mac-like, user-friendly, mouse interface to MS-DOS production programs. The Design-A-Form feature allows user to create their own input forms and reports. The companion Studio Budget program features self-designed detail sheets; pop-up features such as a clipboard (notebook); sideways printing; a window to DOS and detailed help throughout the program. Program supports unlimited data size and detailed comparisons allow cost tracking .

Price: Scheduling $695, Budgeting $695 or both for $1250. Security Key Module $100.

FILM WORKS
Carlan, Graham & Associates, Inc.
12210 Nebraska Avenue
Suite 51
Los Angeles, California 90025
Tel. 213/820-3833
FAX 213/207-1330

Minimum System Requirements:
Macintosh: Not Available
MS-DOS: 400K RAM, 10MB Hard Drive or 2-Double Sided High Density Floppy Drives. Mouse and graphics adaptor not required.

Program Description: This program—the newest on the market— introduced a very user-friendly interface without a mouse. Four function keys provide instant topical help screens, access to pop-up lists, list modification, copying repeated data and a pop-up calculator, which places results in numeric fields. Program prints strips on plain paper or can use Movie Magic strip holders. The Budget program will also read Movie Magic and Toolkit files. The company provides 24 hour, seven days a week telephone support (via pager) and a user bulletin board system.

Price: Scheduling $600; Budgeting $600. Ten percent discount to DGA members.

MACTOOLKIT
606 Wilshire Blvd. - Suite 604
Santa Monica, CA 90401
Tel. 213/395-4242
FAX 213/393-7747

Minimum System Requirements:
Macintosh: Mac Plus
MS-DOS: Not available

Program Description: Originally a Macintosh version of FILM PRODUCTION TOOLKIT, the program is now independent with many original features. The program uses the Macintosh user-friendly interface. The schedule program includes pull-down lists for all breakdown fields which reduces typing by allowing you to add items in any field by clicking a mouse button. The Design-A-Form feature allows users to create their own input forms and reports. The new Storyboard feature allows printing storyboard frames on special, wide-board strips. The companion budget program includes enhanced globals; a detail maker which allows designing of sheets for sets, effects, etc; and cost tracking. A new Rate Book on disk utility, published in association with The *Hollywood Production Manual* is available.

Price: Scheduling $695; Budgeting $695 or $1350 for both.

MOVIE MAGIC
Screenplay Systems, Inc.
150 East Olive Avenue - Suite 305
Burbank, CA 91502
Tel. 818/843-6557
FAX 818/843-8364

Minimum System Requirements:
Macintosh: MacPlus with 1 MB RAM, two disk drives.
MS-DOS: 1 MB RAM, 80286 CPU, 10 MB Hard Drive. Mouse
and graphics adaptor (Hercules, EGA or better) required.

Program Description: A graphics mode program which features
user-friendly ,Macintosh-like operation in the MS-DOS version
and has a unique, easy to use English language sort utility. The
program uses a new multi-layered database technology which has
a capacity to store 10 sorted orders. The scheduling program
introduced plastic holders (in clear yellow, green, red , blue, purple
and orange) to fit die cut paper strips (available in 11, 15 and 17
inch length sheets) into production boards. Information can be
imported into the breakdown pages from reports compiled by the
companion script formatting program: Scriptor The budget program has a library feature for creating custom rate books and can
compare up to 16 budget versions at once. The company offers
phone support (Monday-Friday, 9am-5pm) regular training classes
and a bulletin board system for user problems.

Price: Scheduling $695; Budgeting $695.

TURBO A.D.
Quantum Films Software
8230 Beverly Blvd. - Suite 17
Los Angeles, California 90048
Tel. 213/852-9661
FAX 213/655-6745

Minimum System Requirements:
Macintosh: Not Available
MS-DOS: 394K RAM, 2-Double Sided Double Density Floppy Drives. Mouse and graphics adaptor not required, but mouse is supported.

Program Description: A text mode program which has additional optional programs: Script Scan and Turbo Reports. Board printing program uses fast text mode to print strips horizontally on a wide carriage printer and "clear" mylar tape which shows the color of standard cardboard strips under the printing. Script Scan reads breakdown information from any word processor script file into the Turbo A.D. schedule. The program allows user to add "marks" in the text for props, vehicles, etc . Marked information is then added to breakdown fields, reducing the amount of typing when inputting schedule information. Turbo A.D. sends some files to the companion, Turbo Budget, program which has an optional program: Cost Tracking CompuRates (a rate book on disk) comes with the budget program for use with the look-up table feature.

Price: Scheduling $395 basic; with/one option $595; with two options $695. Turbo Budget Program, $395. With additional cost tracking program, $595.

ADDITIONAL RETAIL SOURCES

Some of the programs have representatives outside Los Angeles. (I tried to make a list, but found they change too frequently.) When contacting the program manufacturers, ask if they have representation near you, or an 800 number for support. The following list is not all-inclusive, but are stores which cater to the motion picture industry.

FRANKIE CORPORATION
3021 Airport Avenue
Suite 112
Santa Monica, California 90405
Tel. 213/398-3771
FAX 213/698-0174
Represents: Film Works and MacToolkit

POSITIVE COMPUTING
14919 Magnolia Blvd.
Sherman Oaks, California 91403
Tel. 818/981-7901
FAX 818/981-8550
Represents: DotZero,Turbo A.D. & Film Works

THE WRITERS COMPUTER STORE
11317 Santa Monica Blvd.
Los Angeles, California 90025
Tel. 213/479-7774
FAX 213/477-5314
Represents: Movie Magic and Film Works

PRODUCTION SOFTWARE CHECKLIST

The following list was prepared as an aide for comparison shopping.

	PROGRAMS		
CATEGORY	**1**	**2**	**3**
Hardware Requirements			
IBM or compatible, Macintosh	___	___	___
RAM memory (256K, 1 MB, etc.)	___	___	___
Hard Drive? Minimum Size	___	___	___
Run on floppy? (Size)	___	___	___
Mouse (Required or Optional)	___	___	___
Wide and/or narrow carriage			
printer required?	___	___	___
Printers supported:			
Laser	___	___	___
Inkjet			
Dot Matrix—Epson	___	___	___
Hewlett Packard	___	___	___
Okidata	___	___	___
Toshiba	___	___	___
Other	___	___	___
Program Features			
When was the program first			
introduced?	___	___	___
What is the current version number?	___	___	___
What is its release date?	___	___	___
Is this a beta test version?			
What is the customer			
base? (number in use)	___	___	___
Menu type (Pull-down,			
Highlighted, Select Code)	___	___	___
File Capacity	___	___	___
Breakdown pages (Schedule)	___	___	___
Accounts (Budgets)	___	___	___
Automatic backups?	___	___	___
Entering			
Are there quick keys?	___	___	___
Are lists available for repeated			
entries? (Cast, Props, Sets, etc.)	___	___	___
Auto-entry features?	___	___	___
Transfer of information			
between programs	___	___	___

Is entry of information natural
  and/or sequence variable?   _____   _____   _____
How are different versions of
  schedules maintained?   _____   _____   _____
How are different versions of
  schedules compared?   _____   _____   _____
Scheduling Features
  Automatic Sorts   _____   _____   _____
    Number of criteria you may sort on _____ _____   _____
    Are automatic sorts stored?   _____   _____   _____
    Is sorting language easy to
      understand?   _____   _____   _____
  Manual sorts (on screen)   _____   _____   _____
    Readability of strip information:
      breakdown strip:readability   _____   _____   _____
    Number of fields visible   _____   _____   _____
    Number of visible variables   _____   _____   _____
  Banners (Day/Week Breaks)   _____   _____   _____
    How are banners and day
      breaks entered?   _____   _____   _____
    Can you combine
      days? (i.e., Days 1-3)   _____   _____   _____
Reports
  Overall look of form printouts?   _____   _____   _____
  Speed of printout   _____   _____   _____
  Are report forms adjustable?   _____   _____   _____
  Are there limits to reports?   _____   _____   _____
  Does program transfer
    information to a Production
    Report?   _____   _____   _____
  Does program transfer information
    to a Callsheet   _____   _____   _____
  Does program print Day-Out-
    Of-Days Day-Out-Of-Days   _____   _____   _____
    Are Drop and Pickups shown?   _____   _____   _____
    Are Start, Work, Hold and Finish
      indicated?   _____   _____   _____
  Does program print strips?   _____   _____   _____
    Printing features (horizontal
      and/or vertical)   _____   _____   _____
    Printout sizes (narrow standard,
    wide standard or outsized)   _____   _____   _____

Special Printout material or stock
   required?   ____   ____   ____

Color stock available?   ____   ____   ____

Does program print location
   room list?   ____   ____   ____

Retail features

Cost of program   ____   ____   ____

Are additional programs required?   ____   ____   ____

What optional programs are
   available?   ____   ____   ____

Package deals?   ____   ____   ____

Return policy?   ____   ____   ____

Lease program?   ____   ____   ____

Security   ____   ____   ____

   Copy protection system
    (key, limited installs,
    security module)   ____   ____   ____

   Number of installs allowed   ____   ____   ____

   Are installs limited (cost of
    new installs)   ____   ____   ____

   Can disk optimizers be used
    once the program is installed?   ____   ____   ____

What are the phone support hours?   ____   ____   ____

Does the company maintain a
   Bulletin Board System?   ____   ____   ____

Are classes available?   ____   ____   ____

Is there on screen help?   ____   ____   ____

Upgrade policy   ____   ____   ____

   (Free for ____ months,
   or cost per upgrade ____)

GLOSSARY

Note: Words in *italics* are defined elsewhere in the glossary.

Actors
Those people who perform the action and say the dialogue as written in the screenplay according to the directions of the director. The main union/guild for actors is the Screen Actors Guild. See *S.A.G.*

Added Scene
When an additional scene needs to be inserted into a script which has already been numbered, instead of re-numbering all the following scenes, a letter is added, e.g., Scene 23-A.

Animals
When used in motion picture filming, animals require special handling, handlers, trainers, wranglers, etc. Many times, look-a-like animals will be used if the scene requires special tricks or actions.

Art Department
The department of a motion picture crew which is responsible for creating the "look" of a film. Staff usually includes an Art Director and/or Production Designer, Assistant Art Director & Draftsperson.

211

Asterisk
Used to indicate make-up and hair references when breaking down a script.

Atmosphere
See *extras.*

Atmosphere Cars
Any car, truck, motorcycle, etc., which is used in a scene on the production and is not used by the *principal players* or any of the *speaking parts.*

Auditors
That person assigned to account for the money spent on the production. (aka, Location Auditors, Production Accountants.)

Bits
(see *silents*)

Breakdown
(aka Script Breakdown) When prepared by the UPM or First A.D., it is a detailed analysis of each and every element needed to shoot a motion picture. Script Supervisors also prepare breakdowns, but for timing purposes.

Breakdown Sheet
A form used in breaking down the script into its individual elements, color-coded as follows: Day Exterior-Yellow, Night Exterior-Green, Day Interior-White and Night Exterior-Blue. See *Chapter Four.*

Budget Form
A detailed form which lists all the elements needed to make a film, the amount of time they will be needed and how much they will cost.

Camera Car
A specially-designed vehicle which holds the camera, its operator and usually the Director and Camera Assistant to film a
travelling vehicle, person or to get *running shots* or *run-bys.*

Camera Mount Car
A special mount which allows the camera to be attached to an
automobile for the purposes of filming the action either inside
the car, or as the car is moving. (See also *camera car, front car
mounts, side car mounts*).

Camera Operator/Helicopter
Sometimes, it is necessary to hire a special camera operator who
is specially trained in filming motion pictures from helicopters.
He will work closely with the helicopter pilot to get all necessary shots.

Cast
The performers appearing in a production. On a budget form,
"Cast" refers specifically to all the actors, but not the *extras.*

Character
The name of the person an actor portrays in the production.

Child Actors
Any actor under the age of 18. There are strict rules governing
the working hours/conditions, etc., of Child Actors. Usually,
a teacher or welfare worker will be required. Check with *S.A.G.*
for latest rules.

Circle
Used to indicate wardrobe when breaking down a script.

Close
Camera's POV will be in very close to the subject matter. Also
see *close-up.*

Close-up
A shot of an actor in which you see mainly his head and shoulders.

Color-Coding
A system for simplifying the breakdown process. The first color code system is for the *breakdown sheets* themselves, and the second for the individual categories on the *breakdown sheets.* See Chapter Four.

Completion Bond Company
A company which, for a contracted fee usually based on a percentage of the budget, agrees to step in and pay the costs necessary to complete the production in the event the production goes over budget. It is customary for the completion bond company to then step in and closely oversee the production until it is finished.

Copter Mount
A special platform on a helicopter which holds the camera, e.g. Tyler Mount.

Cover Set
In the event of a sudden change of plans (actor is sick, weather is wrong for the exterior planned, etc.) this is an easily controllable, and sometimes moveable, set which can be shot without losing a day's work.

Coverage
All the shots necessary from all angles and *set-ups.* For example, if two actors are talking to each other, the director will want a *master shot* and coverage of the actors talking and listening to each other.

Crane
(aka Whirly) A large wheeled support which carries the camera on an arm which pivots. There are places for the director,

camera operator, and camera assistant to sit, and a trolley for the boom.

Crew

The term used to refer to all the technical and production people who work behind the camera to make a motion picture or television show.

Cut To

A phrase used to indicate that one scene should end and the next begin abruptly without the use of an *optical effect* such as a *fade, dissolve,* etc.

C.Y.A.

Cover Your Ass. One of the three Basic Rules. See Chapter Two.

Dailies

(aka Rushes) The scenes which were shot the previous shooting day and then screened for the producer, director, editor and others.

Dawn

It is important that "Dawn" and not "Day" be indicated on the breakdown sheet (shooting schedule, script, etc.) to indicate the specific of the action, as it implies a certain look (long shadows, pale light, etc.)

Day

What should be marked in the appropriate place on the breakdown sheet (shooting schedule, script, etc.) to indicate the time of day of the action. On the production strips, it is abbreviated, 'D'.

Day Players

The actors in the film who may have only a few lines or a few scenes. They are underlined in red in the script and noted in the "Cast - Speaking" box on breakdown sheets.

Day Shots
Those scenes in the production which are to be shot in daylight —either real or artifical, interior or exterior.

Day-For-Day
Shooting Day scenes during actual daylight hours.

Day-For-Night
Although night interiors can usually be shot during the day by dressing the windows, night exterior filming during the day requires special filters to make it appear as if the scenes were shot at night.

Deleted Scene
When a scene needs to be deleted from a script which has already been numbered, instead of re-numbering all the following scenes, simply mark, "Scene 24 - Omitted."

Director
Hired by the producer, the director is the person responsible for all the creative aspects of a motion picture or television show.

Director of Photography
The person responsible for the lights on the set and photography of the project, under the supervision of the director.

Dissolve
An optical effect which makes it seem as if one scene is literally dissolving into the next scene. See also *Optical Effect.*

Dolly
A wheeled platform which holds the camera and its operator for moving shots. Various kinds are: Western, Crab, Elemac, etc.

Double Move
A move away from a location, and then back to it. Generally, this is an expensive way of shooting and should be avoided. There are exceptions: See Chapter Seven.

Dress

To change the appearance of an item so that it can be used on the set. For example, "dress the windows for night" means to change the look of the windows so that it will appear to be nighttime outside.

Drop-and-Pick-Up

When there are at least 10 free days between the day an actor last works and the next day he works on the same show, he may be dropped off salary and picked up again later. Can only be done once per show per actor.

Dummy

A life-size doll used to double a real actor in an extremely dangerous, or potentially dangerous, scene.

Dusk

It is important that 'Dusk' and not 'Night' be indicated on the breakdown sheet (shooting schedule, script, etc.) to indicate the specific of the action, as it implies a certain look (long shadows, warm light, etc.)

DOP

English and Australian abbreviation for Director of Photography.

DP

Abbreviation for Director of Photography.

Establishing Shot

Usually a long or full shot which identifies the location and sets the mood for the other shots.

Executive Producer

Generally refers to the person, or company, who has provided the financial resources for the production, although the title can be given for various other reasons to other people on the production.

Extras
Background atmosphere actors. Some extras are members of the *Screen Extras Guild.* In New York, they are members of *Screen Actors Guild.*

Fade In
The phrase used in a script at the beginning of a sequence to indicate that the scene should emerge from total darkness. See also *fade out.*

Fade Out
The phrase used in a script at the end of a sequence to indicate that the scene should disappear into total darkness. (aka Fade To Black).

Financiers
Those people/companies who put up the money necessary to make the motion picture or television project.

First Unit
The main shooting crew for a project, as opposed to Second Unit.

Forced Call
When an actor/crew member is brought back to work before having the minimum amount of time-off, and is paid a "forced call penalty payment."

Front Car Mounts
Special camera mounts which are placed on the front of the car. See *camera mounts.*

Gaffer
The chief electrician on the set who is responsible for setting the lights according to the instructions of the director of photography. The gaffer supervises his electrical crews' positioning of lights.

Gofer

(aka P.A. or Production Assistant). A slang term for a person on a production who does errands for (goes for) the producer, director, production manager, etc. Many production executives have begun their careers as gofers.

Head Board

(aka Header) The first strip on the production board. It is usually about 4 inches wide and contains all the information particular to a show. See Chapter Five.

Helicopter Pilot/Special

To fly, a helicopter with a camera mounts takes a helicopter pilot specially trained in motion picture filming, who will be able to work with the *camera operator* to get the necessary shots quickly and expertly.

Helicopter With A Camera Mount

A helicopter that has a special platform for the camera, e.g., Tyler Mount (aka 'Copter mount).

High Angle

Camera's POV for shooting will be elevated. Usually this notation implies that a crane will be used. See also *crane.*

High Full Shot

Generally implying a crane shot with the subject matter in the center of the frame and a good deal of foreground and background.

Holding Board

A two-panel board used when marking the strips. It is generally advisable to complete all strips for a scene/sequence before moving them from the holding board to the *production board.*

Holding Days
The days when an actor is not required to be on-camera, but still has some other filming left to complete. See also *drop-and-pick up.*

In-Town Picture
Usually refers to Los Angeles or New York, where home-based crews will not have to travel "to Location." Schedules are generally five-day work weeks. See also *location picture.*

Independent Producer
Generally, it refers to a producer or production company who is not tied to a major studio for financing.

Insert
A shot which is done earlier or later (sometimes by Second Unit) and then "inserted" into the film in the editing period.

Insurance Company
The company (or companies) who have agreed to provide the multitudinous types of insurance coverage necessary when making a feature or television project.

Location Manager
That person on the production staff responsible for finding and securing all the necessary locations which will be used in the production. Depending on the city, these people may be members of the *D.G.A.* or *I.A.T.S.E.*

Location Picture
When the *cast* and *crew* have to travel away from the production company's home based. Schedules are generally six-day work weeks, and salaries are higher. Most times per diems/expenses are paid.

Main Titles
Generally the front credits at the beginning of a film.

Make-Up
Any reference to make-up for the actors which is mentioned in the screenplay. When doing a breakdown, it should be marked with an asterisk and noted in its appropriate column.

Master Shot
The main shot of the entire action. See also *coverage.*

Matching
When editing, if care and attention to detail has not been paid to make sure that all make-up, hair, weather conditions, costumes, camera angles are in continuity, it will be jarring to the viewer as it doesn't match.

Meal Penalty
When actors and/or crew work more than the prescribed number of hours without having time-off for a meal, they are paid a penalty payment called a "meal penalty."

Medium Shot
A shot of the subject matter so that its entire image is clearly seen and not cut up, as in a *close shot,* or with a lot of foreground or background, as in a Long Shot.

Moving View
A shot which requires action, but generally implies a dolly—not a *camera car.*

Night
What should be marked in the appropriate place on the breakdown sheet (shooting schedule, script, etc.) to indicate the time of day of the action. On the production strips, it is abbreviated, 'N'.

Night Shots
Those scenes in the production which are to be shot at night —either interior or exterior. Unless it is necessary to show the

windows of the interior, most Night Interiors are scheduled to be shot *day-for-night.*

Night-For-Night
When it is not possible to shoot *day-for-night,* then night exteriors (and certain night interiors) will be shot Night-For-Night.

Off-Camera
Any action or dialogue which is not seen by the camera, but is heard by the audience.

On-Camera
Any action which is seen by the camera.

Optical Effect
Any effect which is added by the lab, such as a *fade, dissolve, wipe,* etc.

Out-Of-Sequence
Usually, for expedience sake and budgetary reasons, motion pictures are not shot in chronological order. Scenes are arranged according to the 14 *parameter factors.* See Chapter Six.

Over-The-Shoulder Shot
A shot appearing to be taken from "over the shoulder" of one actor when talking to another. Also see *coverage.*

Page Count
When preparing breakdown sheets, the script is divided into eighths—the smallest allowable portion being one-eighth. Scene length is referred to in x-number of eighths.

Panel
When describing the length of a Production Board, it is usually referred to by the number of panels, each panel being 10 wide and either 15 or 18-¼ inches high. THE CONVERSATION requires at least 8 panels.

Parameter Guides
(aka Parameter Factors) A set of 14 points to be considered, in order, when arranging and re-arranging the strips on the *production board* so as to arrive at the most efficient and cost-effective schedule. See Chapter Six.

Penalty
When certain union/guild rules are violated—intentionally or unintentionally—an additional sum of money will be paid to the person. The most usual penalties are *forced calls* and *meal penalties.*

Period Piece
When the time period of a screenplay is not present day, it is said to be a "period piece."

Photo Double
See *stunt photo double.*

Picture Cars
Any car, truck, motorcycle, etc., which is used in a scene on the production.

Plays
To appear, or to look on camera. "Let's see how this scene plays" means that the director wants to see how that particular scene looks. On a *production board,* it means "to be scheduled."

Practical
Anything on a set which actually works, e.g. *practical sink.*

Practical Sink
One which actually works on a set.

Pre-Recorded
To record any sort of music/effects/dialogue before it is actually filmed. Generally done in pre-production.

Pre-Light
Work done in advance by the electrical department, such as replacing the flourescent bulbs, before the crew comes in to shoot.

Pre-Rig
Work done in advance, such as putting up scaffolding, ceiling mounts, etc., before the crew comes in to shoot.

Primary Locations
The main or extremely special locations in a film. For example, "Union Square" is a primary location whereas 'McNaught's Office" is a *secondary location.*

Principal Photography
That portion of time scheduled to shoot all the scenes in the project. Sometimes, due to certain restrictions (weather, etc.) Second Unit is scheduled before commencement or after completion of principal photography.

Principal Players
The leads in the film, e.g., Harry Caul, Ann and Mark are considered Principals. They are underlined in red in the script and noted in the "Cast - Speaking" box on *breakdown sheets.*

Process Shots
A shot taken against a moving or still background of previously shot footage which is projected onto a transparent screen behind the current action which is being filmed.

Producer
The person exercising overall control over the production of a motion picture (or television show) and ultimately responsible for the show's success or failure.

Production Manager
The producer's executive assigned to the production, responsible for coordinating and supervising all administrative and

technical details of the production, and overseeing the activities of the entire crew.

Production Notes
That space on the breakdown sheet reserved for special notations such as, "technical advisor," "interpreter," "Christmastime setting," etc.

Production Strip Board
The scheduling tool used by Production Managers and First A.D.'s to determine exactly how long it will take to shoot the production. Scene information is marked on strips which are then arranged and rearranged so that they show the most efficient and cost effective way to shoot the picture. The colors of the strips correspond to the Breakdown Sheets.

Production Strips
Made of cardboard, strips are either 15 or 18-1/4 inches long and fit into panels of a Production Strip Board. The strips are color-coded to match the *breakdown sheets*. See Chapter Five.

Prop
Short for Property—any portable object which is used in a scene by one of the actors.

Property Department
That department which is responsible for the manufacturer and/or purchase of all props used on the production.

Re-Dress
To change the look of a location or set. See *dress.*

Run-Bys
A travelling shot which differs from a *running shot* in that the subject matter travels past a stationary camera.

Run-Of-Show-Deal
A deal made for the services—usually of an actor/actress—for a specific salary for a specific number of weeks, no matter how many days the actor/actress works during that time.

Running Shot
A moving shot in which the camera travels at the same pace as the moving subject—person, car, etc., or is attached to the moving subject. Many times a hand-held camera is used for running shots of actors.

S.A.G.
Abbreviation for Screen Actors Guild, the collective bargaining union for actors who work in film (as opposed to videotape).

Scene Name
The identifier which describes the location of the action of the scene, e.g., "Union Square".

Script Breakdown
See *breakdown.*

Second Assistant Director
A DGA designated position on the crew who reports to the *first A.D.* and the *production manager* and is generally responsible for all the *cast* and *extras.* Can be up-graded on *second unit* to *first A.D.*

Second Camera
An additional camera used to film additional sequences at the same time as the *first camera.* a second camera is generally used in scenes which are difficult to re-stage.

Second Unit
A separate filming unit which shoots scenes generally not involving principal players. Although Second Unit can be shot during *principal photography,* it is not unusual for it to be shot either before or after.

Second Unit D.P.
A cameraman who is hired to direct the photography of scenes which have fallen into the second unit listing. Shots which the first unit does not have time to complete, shots which are very complicated or require special skills or equipment (e.g., under-water scenes), or shots which are at a distant location are all examples of when a Second Unit Director of Photography could be hired. Many times, the First Unit Camera Operator and Assistant Cameraman are *up-graded* and moved to Second Unit for the necessary shots.

Secondary Locations
As with *principal players,* and *supporting actors,* there are locations which are deemed more important—*primary locations*—than others, Secondary Locations.

S.E.G.
Abbreviation for Screen Extras Guild, the collective bargaining union for *extras* who work in film (as opposed to video tape).

Sequence
Any grouping of scenes which occur in the same location with the same theme, e.g., "Harry's Warehouse Sequence," "Union Square Opening Sequence," "Surveillance Sequence," etc.

Set Dressing
Any item which is used in the decor of the set, and is not a prop. See also *prop*.

Set-Up
The placement of the camera for a shot. Each time the camera is moved is another "set-up."

Shooting Schedule
A detailed list of everyone and everything needed to shoot a particular scene. Compiled from information on the *breakdown sheets* and the *production board,* it is arranged in shooting order. See Chapter Nine.

Side Car Mounts
Special camera mounts which are placed on the sides of the car.
See *camera mounts.*

Silent Bits
See *silents.*

Silents
An actor who performs an action in a scene which in some way
affects either the direction of the story or the *principal players*
in the scene is a Silent; e.g., a waiter who spills soup on the lead.

Singles
When shooting *coverage* of a scene, a director will want to get
close-up shots of each actor, talking and listening. These close-
ups are called "Singles."

Slow Motion
An effect achieved by running the film through the camera at
a faster than normal speed (or through a projector, slower than
normal.) When shooting, requires a special *variable speed motor.*

Speaking Part
Any actor who utters one single word of dialogue is considered
to have a Speaking Part. They are underlined in red in the script
and noted in the "Cast - Speaking" box on the breakdown
sheets.

Special Camera Operator
To operate a "Panaglide" or "Steadicam" requires a specially
trained camera operator.

Special Effects
Any effect which is special and must be created. See Chapter
Four.

228

Special Effects Department
That division of the production crew, or sometimes a separate independent company, which is in charge of producing all the Special Effects on a production—from STAR WARS, to a practical sink.

Special Portable Camera
To shooting scenes which would not be possible with a standard camera, for example a chase scenes on foot, Panaglide and Steadicam (two brand names) are mounts which allow the camera to mount on the operator's body.

Standard Script Format
As illustrated in Chapter Three, there is a preferred way to type a motion picture screenplay. If other formats are used, it can affect your calculations in judging how much time it will take to shoot.

Started
Usually refers to the first day an actor works. As there are many rules governing an actor once he begins work, the proper start date is very important. See *drop-and-pick up, run of show, upgrade.*

Strike
To remove any equipment used in the shooting of a scene after the shooting has been completed. It is advisable not to strike a set until the *dailies* have been checked and approved.

Stunt Coordinator
The member of the crew responsible for the organization and coordination of the execution of all the stunts on a production.

Stunt Doubles
A stunt person who physically resembles a particular actor and performs any dangerous or potentially dangerous action for

that actor. For example, Mr. C is doubled in the burning Mercedes Benz sequence.

Stunt Photo Double
A stunt person who closely resembles (or is made to resemble) the actor and takes his place in dangerous or potentially dangerous scenes.

Supporting Players
The second leads in the film, e.g., Stanley, Paul, Martin, etc., are considered to be Supporting Players. They are underlined in red on the script and noted in the "Cast—Speaking" box on the breakdown sheets.

Surveillance Equipment
In THE CONVERSATION, the equipment which Harry Caul uses to track Ann and Mark is special, professional equipment which will have to be rented. Most likely, a *technical advisor* will also be hired.

Teacher
See *welfare worker.*

Technical Advisor
A person who is considered to be an expert in a certain field who can ensure the authenticity of a project. In THE CONVERSATION, the operation of the surveillance equipment would be overseen by a Technical Advisor.

Transportation
That department of the crew responsible for transporting the crew and all necessary equipment and vehicles for the production.

Turn-Around Time
The minimum and specific number of free time which must be given before that person may return to work without incurring

a penalty, e.g., an actor must be given 58 hours between completion Friday to start Monday morning

Underline
The recommended method for marking up a script. It is preferable to "highlighting," as the script is still legible when photocopied.

Up-Grade
To move to a higher pay classification. Usually used in reference to an actor. For example, an *extra* might be up-graded to a *silent bit* (or a *day player,* if given dialogue.)

Variable Speed Motor
A special motor which allows filming at rates other than 24 fps. See also *slow motion.*

Vehicles
Any car, truck, motorcycle, etc., which is used on the production. See also *picture cars, transportation.*

Wardrobe
Any item of clothing which is worn by the actors and mentioned in the screenplay. When doing a breakdown, it should be circled and noted in its appropriate column.

Welfare Worker
When a child under a certain age is hired, it is mandatory that a welfare worker teacher also be hired. See *child actors.*

Wide Angle
Camera's POV for shooting will be wider than normal, and may require the use of a wider angle lens.

Wipe
An Optical Effect used when the new scene literally "wipes" the previous scene from the screen. See *optical effect.*

Wrapped
To finish all required shooting: either at a location, for that day (night), or on the picture altogether.

Zoom In
When the camera appears to move toward the subject in a continuous take. This is usually done by using a *zoom lens.*

Zoom Lens
A special lens which allows the operator to move the image either closer or further away without moving the camera position.

Zoom Out
When the camera appears to move away from the subject in a continuous take. This is usually done by using a *zoom lens.*

INDEX

Note: Entries after semicolon indicates a word in the Glossary.

ABOUT THE AUTHOR

Ralph Singleton works in the motion picture industry as a Producer, Director and Production Manager. He won an Emmy-award as producer of the critically acclaimed television series, CAGNEY & LACEY. He directed and produced *Stephen King's Graveyard Shift* for Paramount Pictures, executive-produced *Another 48 HRS.* starring Eddie Murphy and Nick Nolte, co-produced Eddie Murphy's directorial debut, *Harlem Nights,* as well as co-produced another Stephen King project for Paramount—*Pet Sematary.* He was head of production for Francis Coppola's Zoetrope Studios and was Production Manager on *Exposed* (MGM/UA), *One From The Heart* (Paramount), *The Winds of War* (USA) (Paramount), *History of the World—Part I* (20th Century Fox), *Somebody Killed Her Husband* (Paramount), *Kojak* (Universal), etc.

Mr. Singleton worked his way up through the Directors Guild first as a Trainee, then as an Assistant Director and Production Manager, to finally Producer and Director. His credits are impressive and he has been honored with awards such as the Women In Film Award, The Nancy Susan Reynolds Award, The Humanitas Prize as well as two Emmy nominations in addition to his Emmy Award for Best Dramatic Series in 1986.

His credits as assistant director include: *Testament* (Paramount), *The Seduction of Joe Tynan* (20th Century Fox), *Greased Lightning* (Warner Bros.), *Taxi Driver* (Columbia), *Network* (Paramount), *The Front* (Warner Bros.), *Three Days of the Condor* (Paramount), *The Gambler* (Paramount).

He is the only assistant director in the history of the Directors Guild to work on two Academy Award nominated features in the same year, and be nominated for the prestigious DGA Award for both—*Network* and *Taxi Driver*.

Ralph Singleton is also the author of four highly respected books on film production, FILM SCHEDULING; THE FILM SCHEDULING/FILM BUDGETING WORKBOOK; MOVIE PRODUCTION & BUDGET FORMS...INSTANTLY! and the FILMMAKER'S DICTIONARY. He is currently finishing his fifth book, FILM BUDGETING. Mr. Singleton gives seminars on film and television production in the United States for the American Film Institute and in Europe for the Italian-based Forums International.

Mr. Singleton makes his home in Los Angeles, California.